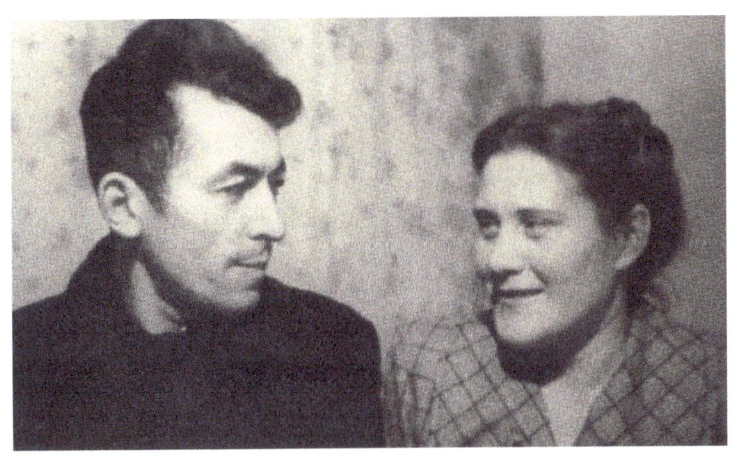

Dedicated to a memory of Nadia Russ parents
Vera Rekina and Ivan Maloletnev

NeoPopRealism STARZ
21st CENTURY ART

Volume II

Erotica as a High Artistic Aspiration
Compendium of New Millennium Art

This book included artworks created by artists from all over the world, united by one theme - erotica. This art was created in the new millennium, but the foreword also Includes paintings produced before year 2000. All of these artworks reflect our lives and are full of love and hate, passion and sorrow, and dreams . . .

What is Erotica?

"The word erotica typically applies to works In which the sexual element is regarded as part of the larger aesthetic aspect. It is usually distinguished from pornography, which can also have literary merit but which is usually understood to have sexual arousal as it main purpose..."

Encyclopedia Britannica

NeoPopRealism Starz Presents

21st CENTURY ART

VOLUME II

Erotica As A High Artistic Aspiration

This Collection Features The Work From:

Andrzej Michael Kawasaki (USA), Sigmund Abeles (USA), Pete Herzfeld (USA), Joseph Borzotta (USA), Milan Kuzica (Czech Republic), Megh (USA), Jacob El Hanani (USA), Paolo Scalera (UK), Shana Calano (USA), R. Gopakumar (India/Bahrain), Don McCormack (USA), Matthew Goglianese (USA), Charles Seligman (USA), Leanne Maloney (USA), Terry Brown (USA), Frederique Krzis- Lorent (France), David DeRosa (USA), Julie Denec (Canada), Mark Schieferstein (USA), Mohammed Yasin Saddique (UK), Viliam Sulik (Slovakia), Stefan Havadi-Nagy (Germany).

FOREWORD by **NADIA RUSS**

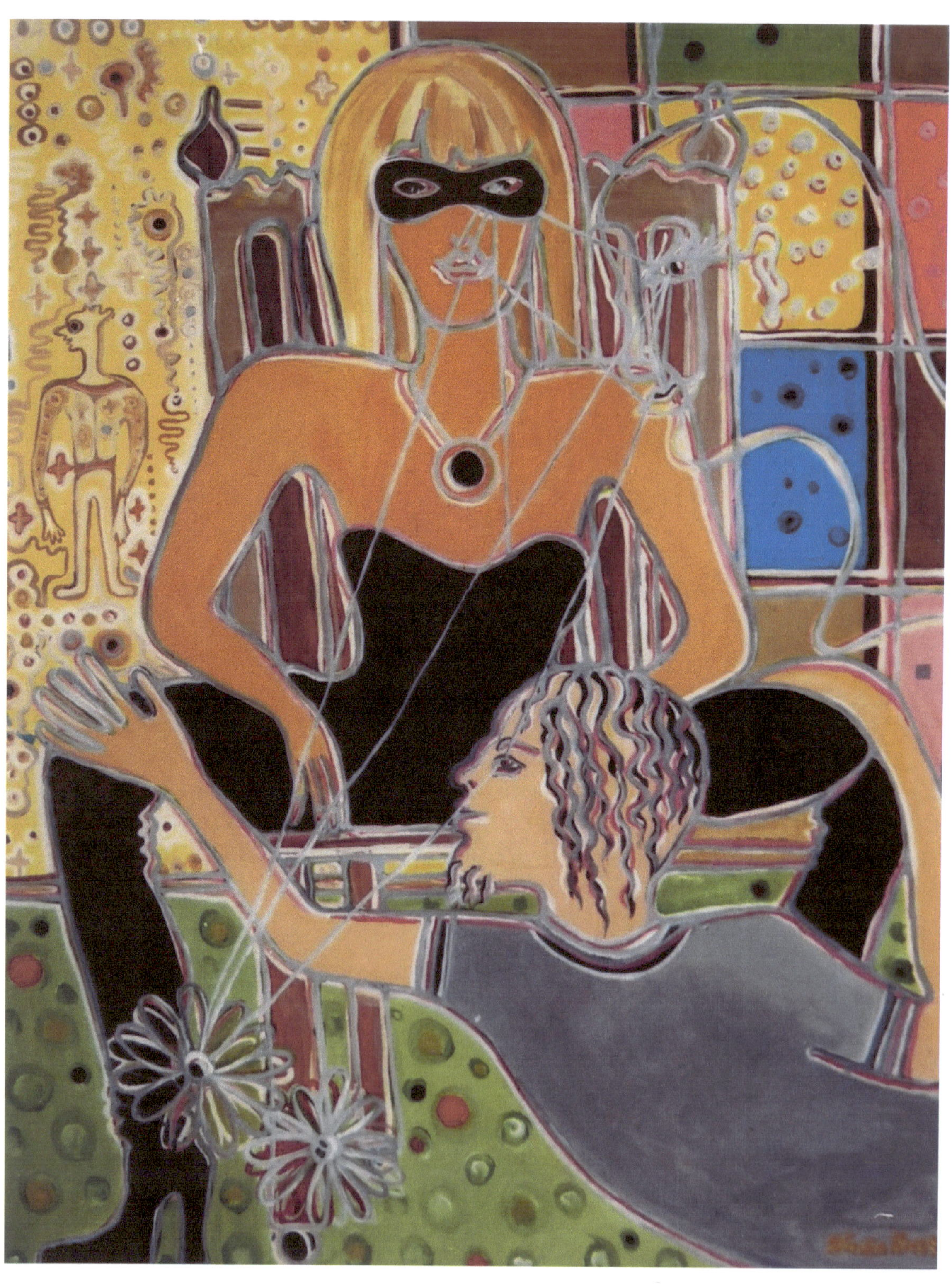

Nadia Russ, *Miss and Her Admirer,* (USA, 2002), acrylic on canvas, 24"x36"
(artwork stolen in Florida)

FOREWORD

by NADIA RUSS

Higher culture and arts always suggest something worthy of attention. The way in which erotica affected and continues affect visual arts is tremendous. This book is intended to trace the role of erotica and erotic symbolism in the visual arts. Erotica has a charm, wit, power of beauty, and aesthetic quality. Erotica and death in art have gone hand in hand since the earliest times. In this book, I will give examples of erotic art, art with explicit and with no explicit depictions of nakedness or eroticism. By the way, the criterion of covert erotica content is still remains unclear . . .

My father, Ivan, was a super-talented man, a professional military by education, communist, and a home tyrant (but soft Inside). He was, by the way, a Stalin's fun. My mother, Vera, was a Christian by belief, sophisticated and beautiful woman with fabulous taste and love to the intellectual freedom. Our home - with reproductions of work of Leonardo D'Vinci and Michelangelo on the walls - was located 50-60 meters from the church of the town of Konotop (East Ukraine). I remember myself as a wild and spoiled child, who often played with other kids at the church's court. These memories remind me a feeling of some mystery, the dark fears of the God's power, and Gogol's fascinating stories about witches and dead souls. I never heard a word sex in our home because my mother and father were innocent people who saw sex as an extension of love and marriage. So do I, even now, with all my sophistication and all kind unwanted experiences.

I left my fabulous fighters - dominating father and fighter for freedom mother - when I was 15, I went to study in Kursk's pedagogical college (music), and after had moved to Moscow.

Since then, I had six abortions (horrible thing to do) and was raped (the date, business colleagues or friends' rape, awful thing) 11 times. One of those rapists was, Minister of Justice, Sergei Lushchikov, and last one in Russia was the local police officer, I do not remember his name. It moved me forward with an idea to leave Russia as soon as possible because I couldn't live any more in country where law and order didn't exist. I sold quickly my apartment at

Zelenogradskaya Street in Moscow and left Russia the same year, 1996.
Now, years later, I still have - like always - my parents' vision at the love and sex subjects: Marriage is following love, and sex is following marriage. And it can't be changed, as it is in my blood.
To me, erotic is Michelangelo's David, it is a spiritualization of human body. It is NeoPopRealist look at this matter, even the most of Americans and the Western Europeans are associating word Erotica with some sexual activities. Opposite, I see erotica (not porn) as an intellectual exploration of human body, with no sexual or minor sexual feelings.
Probably, if my parents saw some images in this book they would be shocked. They were conservative people and lived spiritual live. Personally, I also have a minor interest in a subject of sex, as I feel that the obsession with it only appears as a result of the lack of happiness, stimulating your soul.

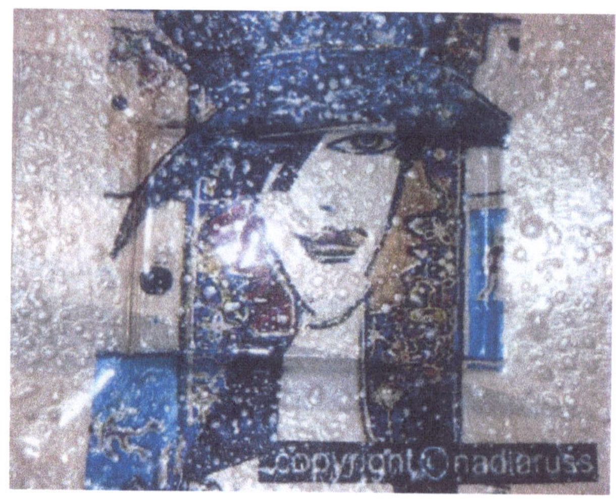

Nadia Russ, *Queen of Magic*, limited edition 7/7, 2006, collectible glass plate 8"x10", lamination on glass

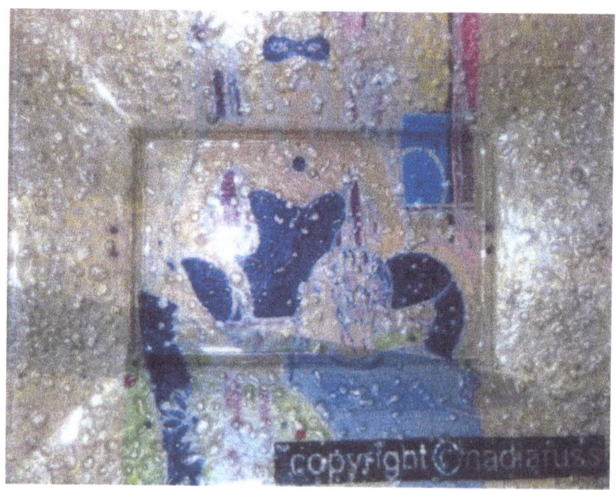

Nadia Russ, *Miss and Her Admirer*, limited edition 7/7, 2006, collectible glass plate 8"x10", lamination on glass. Collection of Kinsey Institute, Indiana University

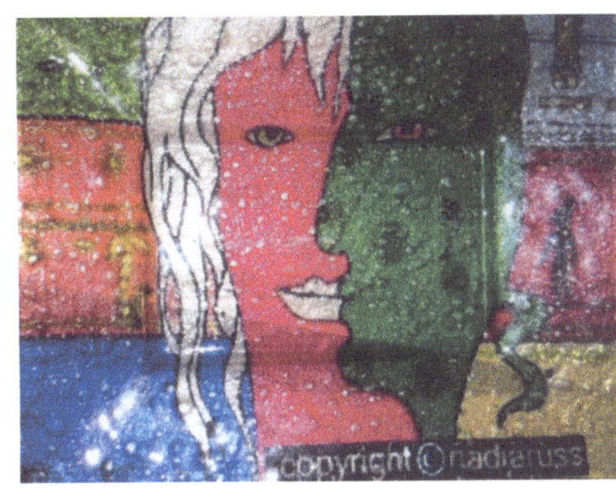

Nadia Russ, *Seasons of Nightmare*, limited edition glass plate 8"x10", 7/7, lamination on glass, 2006

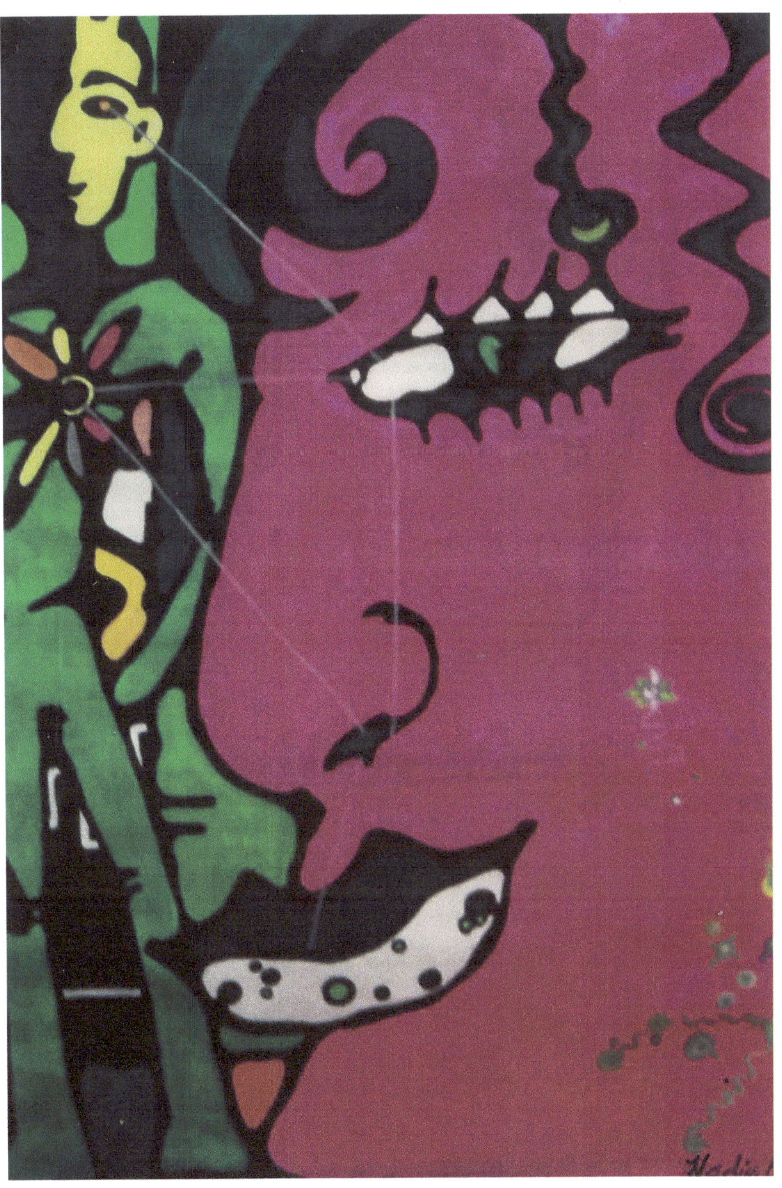

Nadia Russ, *Summer*, 2004, USA, acrylic on canvas. Collection of MOYA, Museum of Young Art, Vienna, Austria

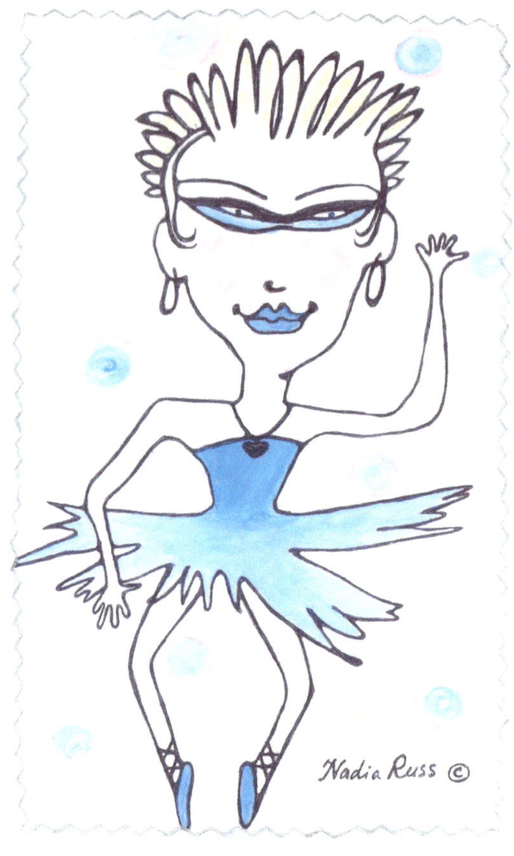

Nadia Russ, *Funky Ballerina*, USA, 2004, ink and acrylic on paper, 5"x10". Print is in collection of D. Burliuk Foundation, Sumy, Ukraine

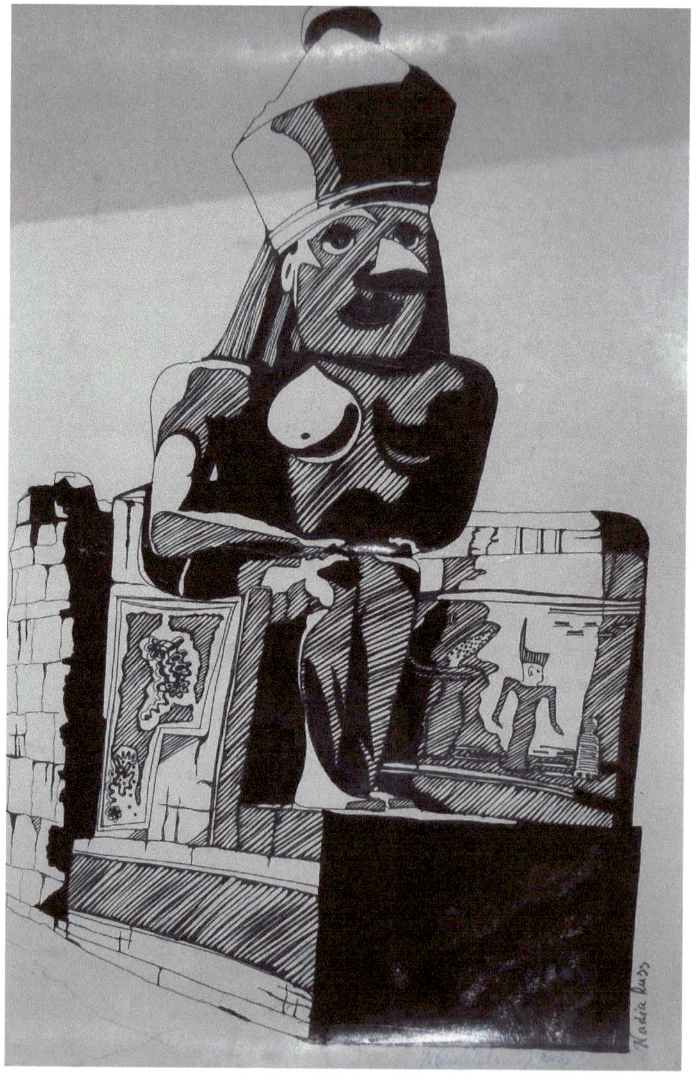

Nadia Russ, *Goddess*, USA, ink on paper, 18"x22"

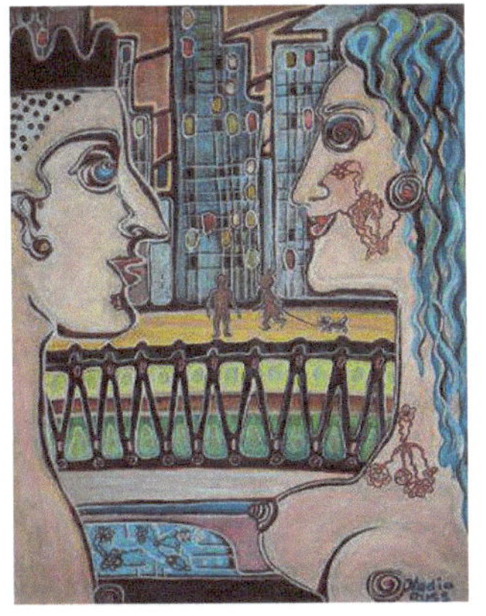

Nadia Russ, *Funny People*, Cyprus, 1996, acrylic on canvas, 50x70 cm

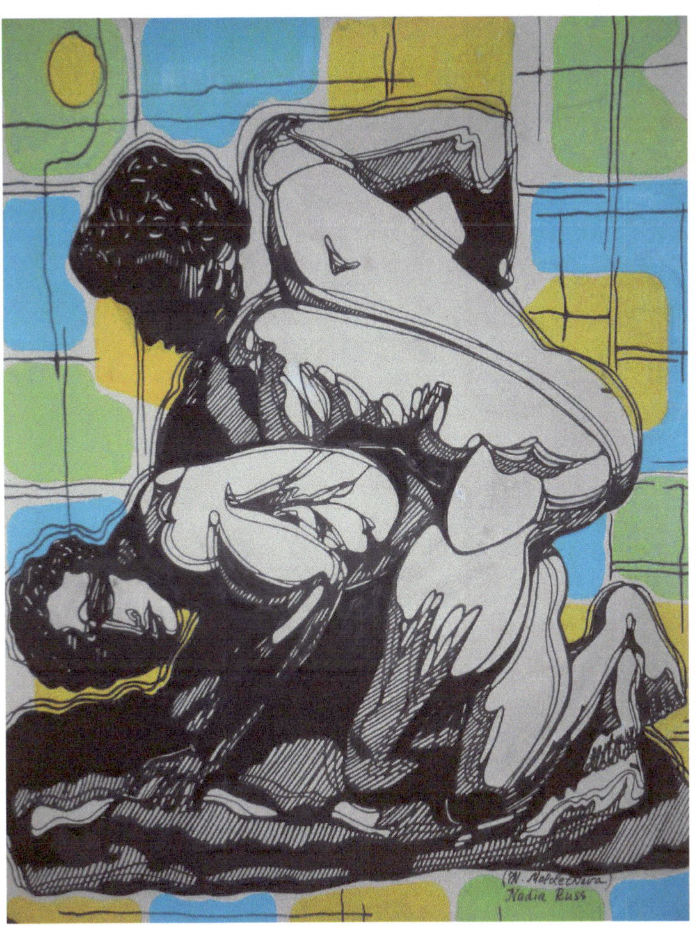

Nadia Russ, *Game is Over*, Bahamas, 1996, ink and acrylic on paper, 22"x26"

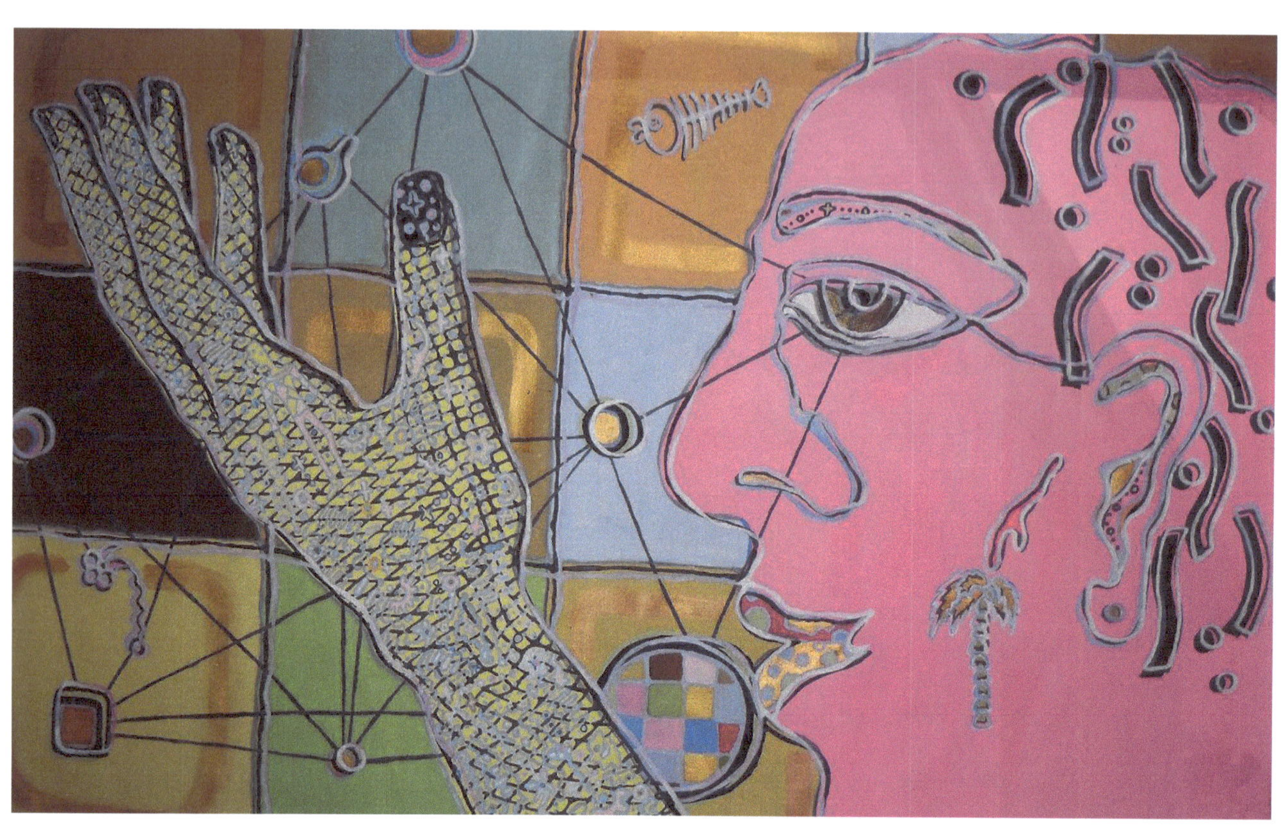

Nadia Russ, *The Hand*, USA, acrylic on canvas, 2007, 41"X70"

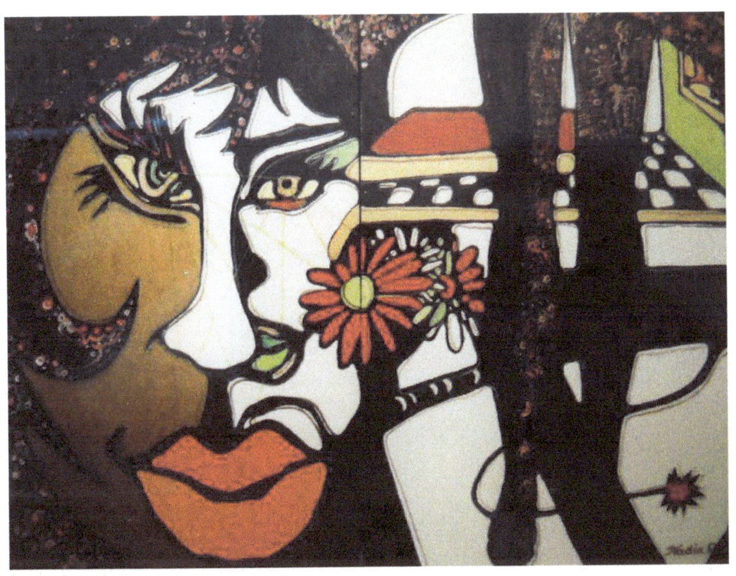

Nadia Russ, *Legs & Fine Man*, 2001, acrylic, two canvases 24"x36" each, (from series of 4). Collection of Kinsey Institute, Indiana University, Bloomington, USA

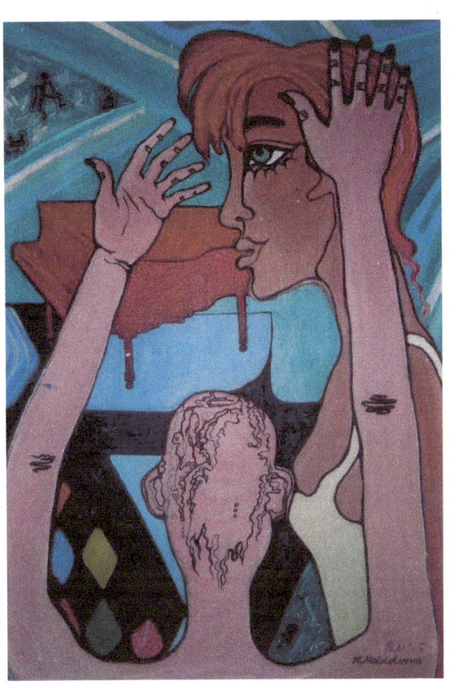

Nadia Russ, *Conductor*, 1996, acrylic/canvas, 24"x36", Bahamas. Collection of Simferopol Art Museum, Ukraine

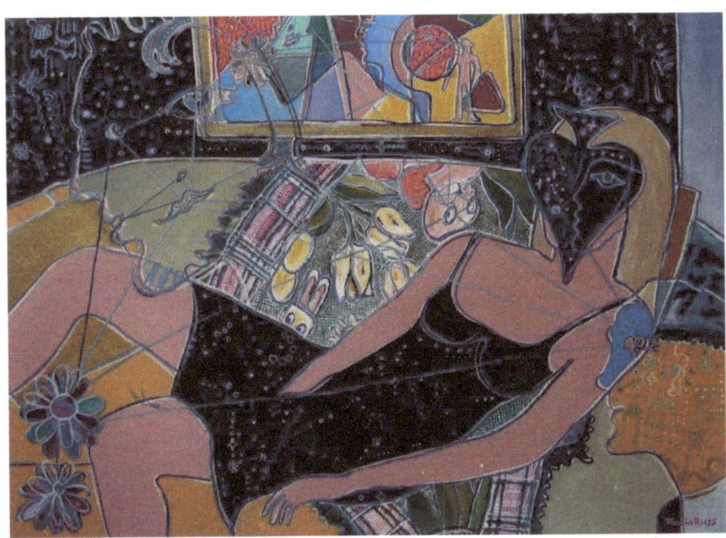

Nadia Russ, *Aces & Faces*, 2002, acrylic/canvas, USA. Collection of Ukrainian Museum in New York City, USA

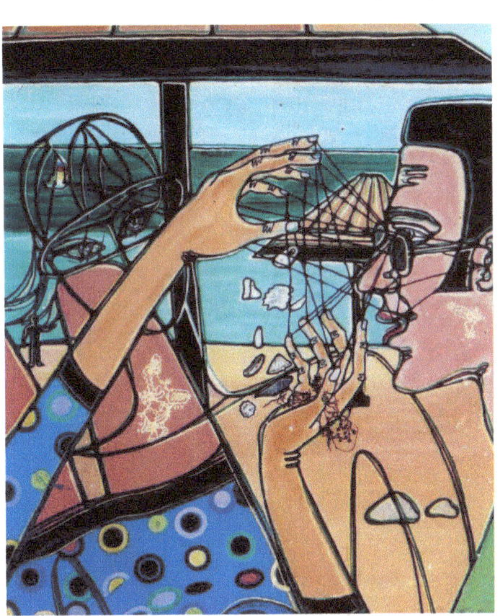

Nadia Russ, *Magic Beach*, 1997, acrylic/canvas, 50"x70", Bahamas. Work is missing in Freeport, Bahamas.

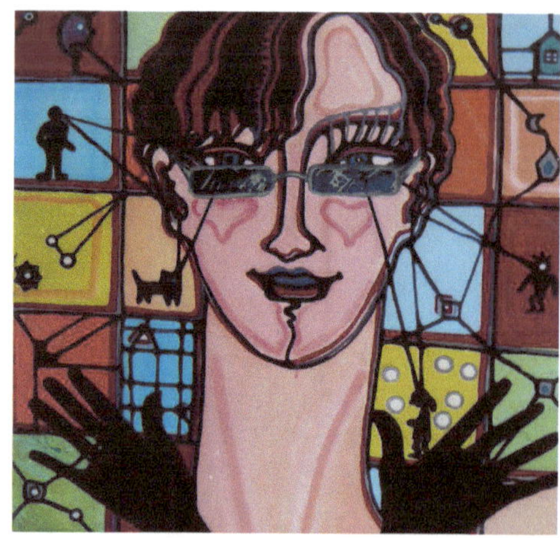

Nadia Russ, *Magician*, 1996, acrylic/canvas, 24"x24". Cyprus. Work is missing in NYC, USA

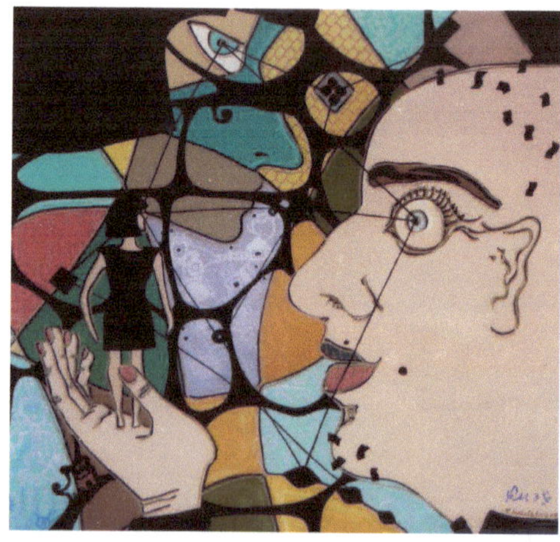

Nadia Russ, *The Game*, 1997, acrylic/canvas, very large size, Bahamas. Work is missing in Freeport, Bahamas

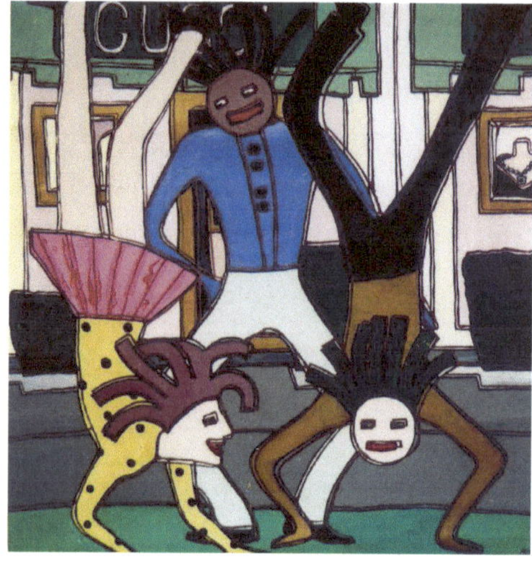

Nadia Russ, *Funny People-Gucci*, 1997, acrylic/canvas, very large size, Bahamas. Work is missing in Freeport, Bahamas

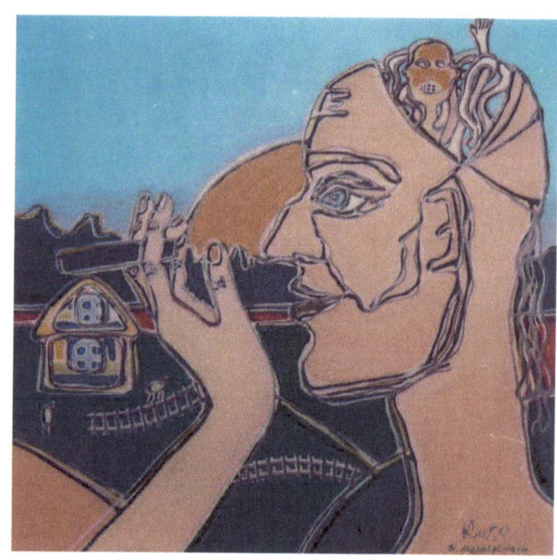

Nadia Russ, *Cigar,* 1997, acrylic/canvas, 24"x24", Bahamas. Work destroyed during art experiments by artist

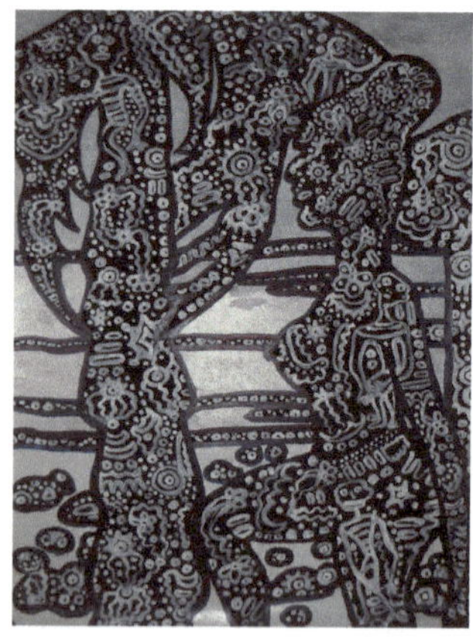

Nadia Russ, *Black Tropics*, 1997, Bahamas, acrylic/paper, 24"x26",

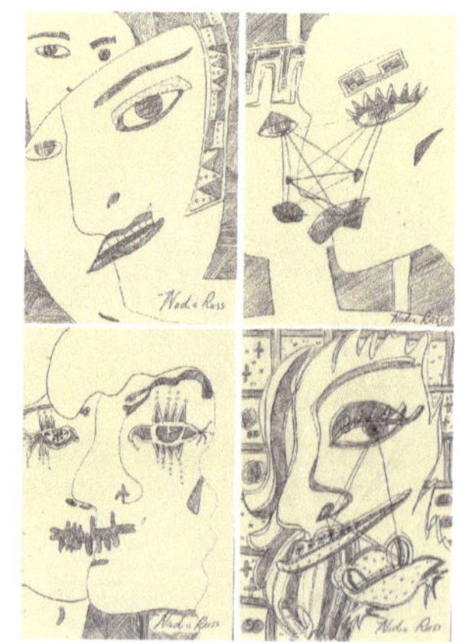

Nadia Russ, *Faces*, 2006, USA, ink/paper, 8"x5" each drawing,

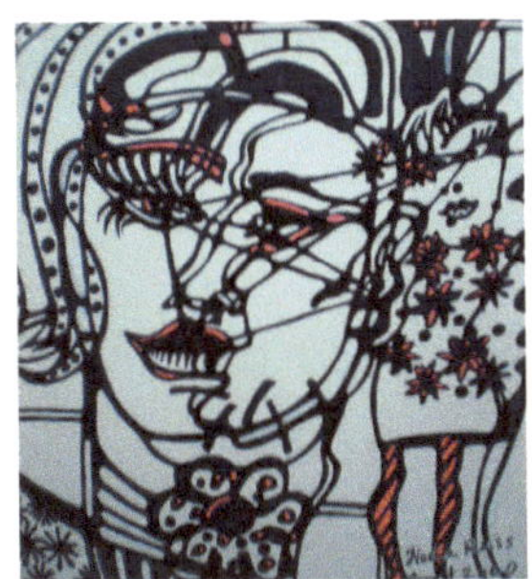
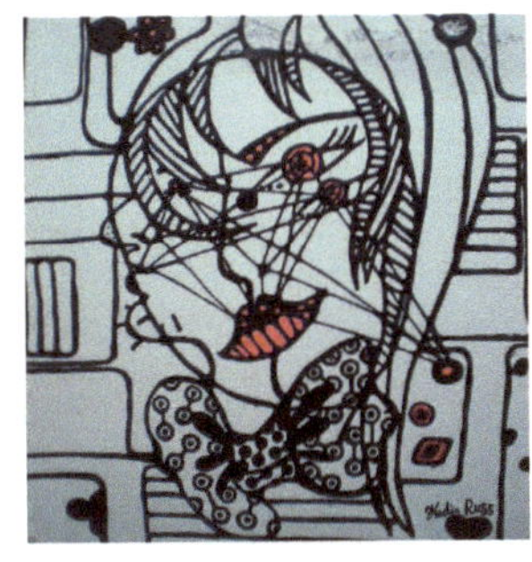
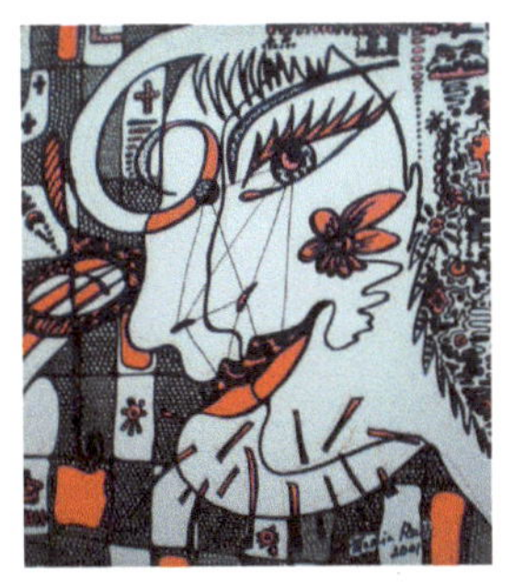
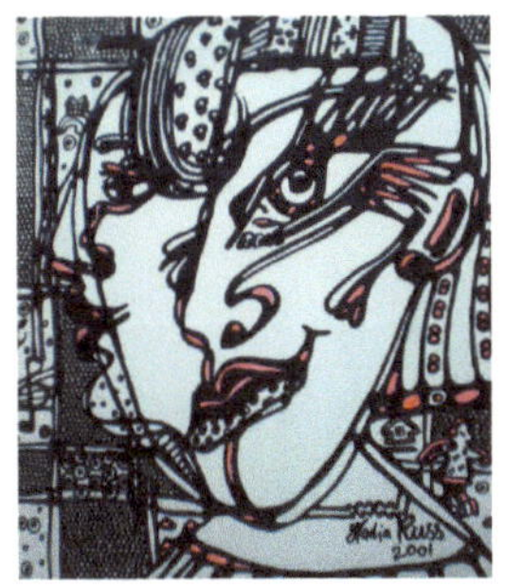

Nadia Russ, *Faces series*, 2000-2001, USA, ink & acrylic on paper, about 22"26" each work

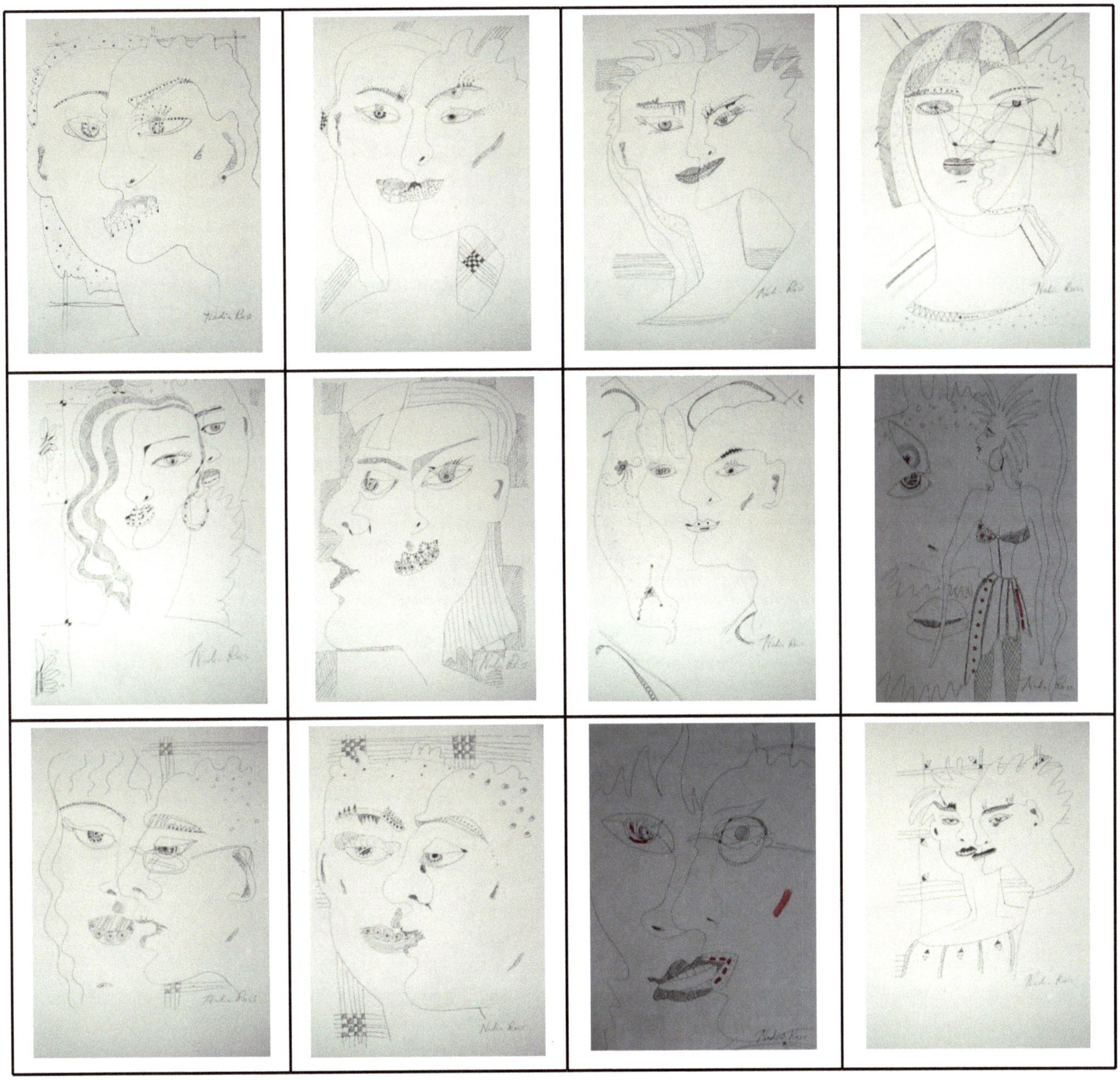

Nadia Russ, *Series Faces*, 2005-2006, USA. Part of permanent collection of Kinsey Institute, Indiana University (Kinsey institute collection has 200 Nadia Russ' ink drawings)

WHAT IS EROTICA?

Regularly, depiction of objects recognized as erotic when they are juxtaposed with human subject, is typical indication. Probably, all art has covert erotic content and being the expression of unconscious erotic fantasies. But not all covertly sexual art is considered erotic. Generally, the erotic art explores ideas and assumptions about the nature and relationships between man and woman, and focuses on an investigation of this subject.

The art is intended to target audience.

In ancient period, there already existed the category of the pornography, the sexually stimulating art. There is the opposition between the erotic and pornographic art. And there is one important philosophical question: how differ an erotic art from pornography. Very often erotic art involves images intended to stimulate sexually, but these images are less explicit than those of pornography. By the way, for example, art works of such superstars artists as Picasso and Dali are as explicit as the open-mined magazines.

What important is how the erotic quality of a painting related to its artistic value. And answer could be: the more erotic artwork is (not becoming a porn), the higher its artistic value is, and other dimensions of the painting's content are important, often it takes a sensitive interpretation to establish.

MEDIEVAL CULTURE, MIDDLE AGES & RENAISSANCE

We can discover many examples of eroticism in medieval art. These appear to be vestigial survivals of the old pagan cults. More generally, erotic art appears in medieval culture as a kind of obbligato to solemn and sacred themes.

We can find it in the elements of ecclesiastical architecture and church furnishing (bosses, capitals of columns, corbels, and misreports ...) In Bristol Cathedral there is a miser cord which is an illustration of the expression 'to lead apes in Hell'. . .

In the church of Saint-Martin (Champeaux) you can see a symbolic illustration of the French proverb 'Petite pluie abat grand vent', which is 'Little rain beats a big wind'. And it is not only examples of erotica to be found in medieval art. Let's look at the fresco of The Last Judgment by Giotto in Arena Chapel at Padua, in the composition is a group of four naked sinners, each suspended by the part through which they have offended - one hands by the hair, another by the tongue, and two others by the sexual organs.

The erotic representation rises during the last phase of the Middle Ages. And one of the artists who created the most interesting works is Hieronymus Bosh.

The Renaissance sometimes is thought of as representing a return to pagan hedonism, after Christian asceticism of preceding centuries. The Birth of Venus by Botticelli with its methodological composition is indeed the embodiment of ideas different from those of Bosh. The erotic element is refined. Botticelli spiritualizes the nude.

A little later in the history of Italian art, we find that Attis-Amor by Donatello wears the open breeches of Attis, which reveal and call attention to his genitals. Also, like Eros, he is equipped with wings. It defies stylistic and the moral assumptions of its time, and constitutes eroticism.

The impact of the Raphael's work Triumph of Galatea with its composition and energy is also erotic.

At the end of 16th century, artists of Europe were creating erotic works for their patrons. One of them is Mannerist Bartholomaus Spranger, court painter to the Emperor Rudolph II in Prague. In his Vulcan and Maia, he created erotic feelings through a use of contrasts, such as the difference in age between the lovers.

The native Indian painters were influenced by European art, Indian erotic art combined realistic material and mythology . .. . .

EROTICA AS A HIGH ARTISTIC ASPIRATION

EROTICA & RELIGIONS

Catholic tradition to believe that human nature is good, and God designed the reproduction process and it is good. The love between man and woman is a sacrament, revelation, a metaphor for God's love for his people and Jesus' love for His Church. Sexual desire between man and woman leads to marriage and often draw them in a renewal of their love.

To appreciate the erotic arts of India, we must understand the role of erotica in the scheme of things according to Hinduism, which is a way of life according to prescribed codes. Every Hindu has to undergo sixteen denotary rituals and four stages of life. The final aim of life is salvation, which is the merging of the individual with the supreme soul. The ancient Indians took a healthy view of all aspects of life and gave erotica its due importance.

Christianity was non-erotic religion (Virgin birth of Jesus . . .). Erotic art was rare In the Early Christian period and the Middle Ages.

The Christian repression of sexuality led to the depiction of erotic horrors in art. Sometimes, the Christian fears of sex were explored in a way that expresses the attractions of what was feared.

Erotica in the visual arts has traditionally repelled or embarrassed Arabs: erotica plays on human sexuality, the pornography is offensive and arousing baser instincts; even in the visual arts they both have high artistic quality. There is the differentiation in two concepts in Arab's culture and the varying attitudes.

Several years ago, Jewish Ortodox Naomi Wilzig has opened the World Erotic Art Museum (WEAM) in Miami Beach (Florida, USA), one of the largest erotic art collections worldwide. Some items are dating from 300 BC. Naomi Wilzig was raised in an environment where there was absolutely no discussion of sex, as it didn't exist. Siggi Wilzig, was one of the founders of the US Holocaust Memorial Museum in Washington. He never shared his wife's passion for erotic art, and she pursued her hobby under the pseudonym Miss Naomi. But most American museums still keep their erotic art collections hidden from the general public.

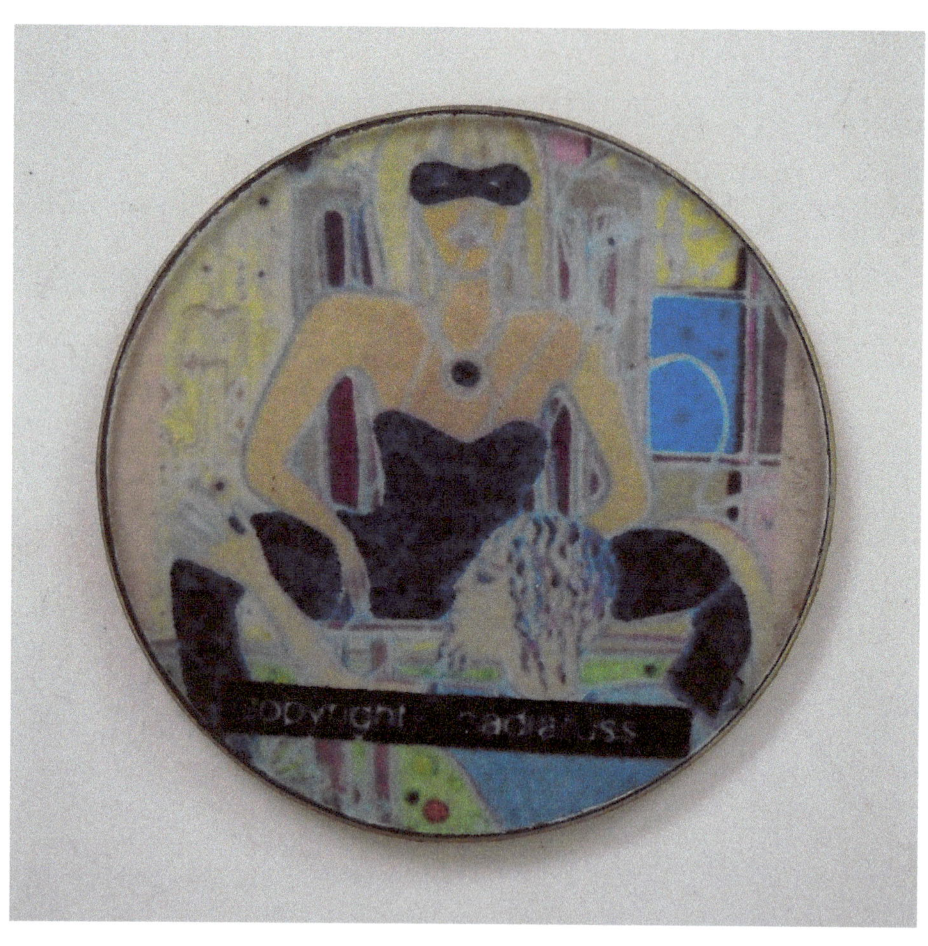

Nadia Russ, *Miss & Her Admirer*, limited edition 1/8 glass disc, lamination, 2006, diameter 4"x4", USA.
Collection of WEAM, Miami Beach, FL, USA

LOVE + GENIUS= EROTICA

Some of the most rhetorically elevated and refined works of Renaissance visual art were produced by artists who explored erotic subjects. In the renaissance art, the theme of carnal, illicit, erotic love provided an endless source of inspiration. Some of the images are even vulgar, some artists explore erotica with learned erudition.

Perino del Vaga, Francesco Salviati, Giulio Romano, and Parmigianino decorated sacred famous liturgical spaces with decorous frescos. At the same time they were exploring in their artwork the subjects such as pederasty and fornication. Marcantonio Raimondi, Raphael's engraver who reproduced the master's most fascinating pictorial inventions, was also producing the most sexually explicit and transgressive works ever appeared in visual arts.

With some erotic art, the avocation of erotic feelings is a secondary aim. Artists may want achieve some further end, such as psychological disorientation, social commentary or simply humor. Then it is an 'instrumentally' erotic art.

The most of erotic drawings, painting, and sculptures were made for private view, and were meant to be enjoyed by a special audience, behind the walls of a studio or private home.

The production of prints was under control by the Church and the government authorities to avoid scandalous among uncontrollable audience . . .

Many art works maybe full of erotic feelings without depicting sexual activity and can be described and discussed in different ways: historical, to place it in the context of the culture and the social situation with aesthetic believes of the time when it was created. Second way is - according to what it seems to express, subject, unconscious and conscious symbolism.

Probably, some images in this book, which contains art works from contemporary artists from all over the globe, could arouse fears, sometimes provoke outrage, sometimes lead to their destruction. Such reaction is due to the fact that our feelings are repressed. The art emphasized political, social, and erotic contexts rather than value, the meaning of artwork. By the way, today, the main subject of Western art is the erotica with its openness to diverse forms.

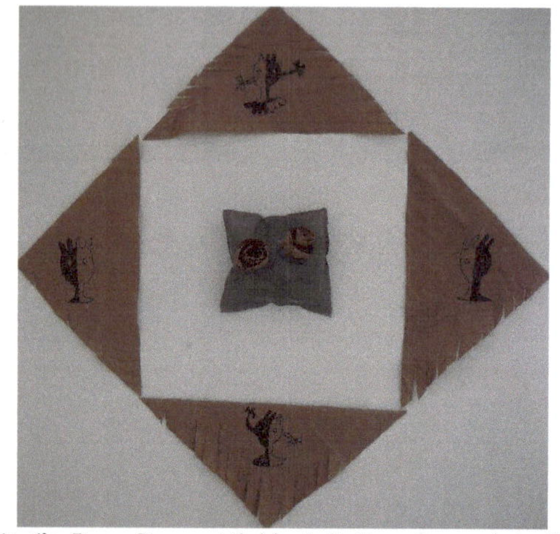

Nadia Russ, *Roses*, Mini-installation, Paper/plastic pillow/ink, 2009, USA

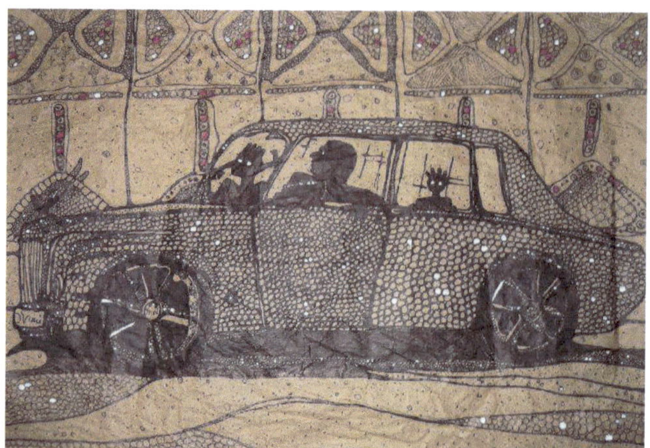

Nadia Russ, *D'Vinci*, ink on paper, 38"x27", 2209, USA

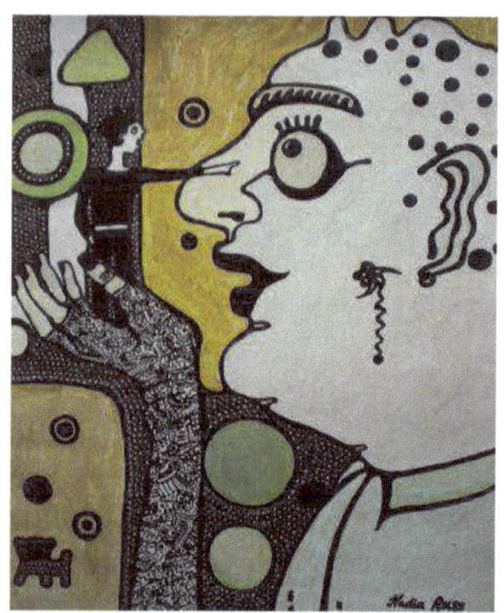

Nadia Russ, *The Game*, ink & acrylic on paper, 22"x26", 2004, USA

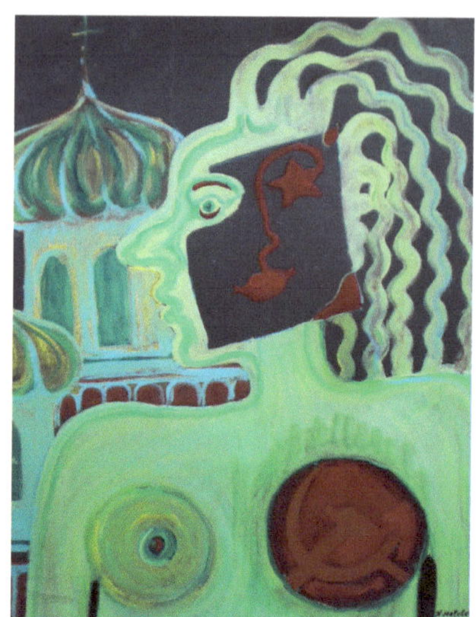

Nadia Russ, *Russian Breast Cancer*, acrylic on paper, 22"x26", 1997, Bahamas

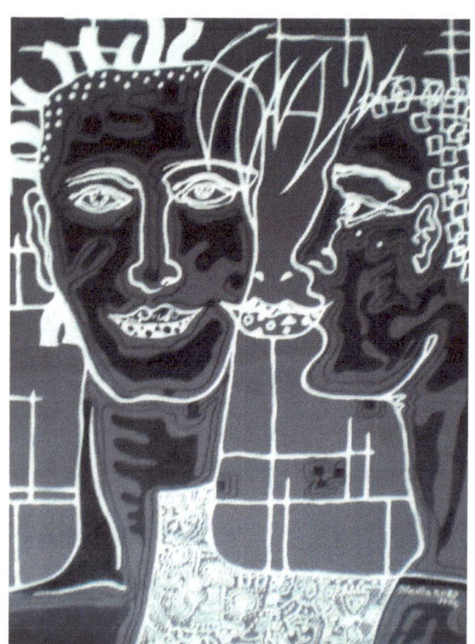

Nadia Russ, *Faces on Black 1*, acrylic/ black paper, 22"x26", 1998, Bahamas

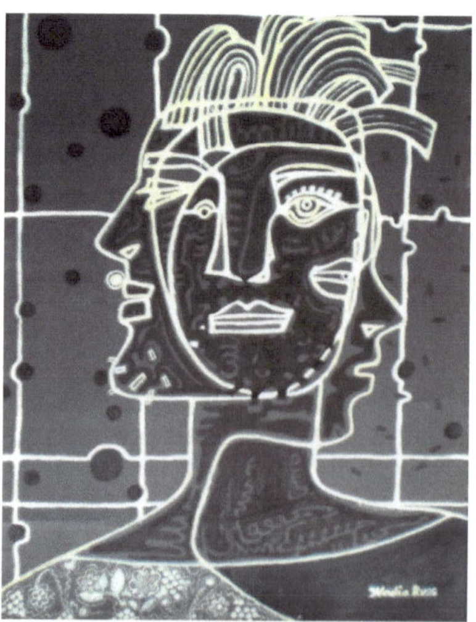

Nadia Russ, *Faces on Black 2*, acrylic/ black paper, 22"x26", 1998, Bahamas

Today In New York

Daily News at Your Service

Thursday, August 3, 2000

With the **first August weekend** looming, it's no time to take summer for granted, so take in one of the seasonal festivals: **the Philharmonic in Van Cortlandt Park, the African Jazz Band at Pier 54, swing dancing in the Harlem Meer. Broadway cast members perform at the Children's Museum and at Bryant Park,** and though this midsummer is already past, take your pick of Pucks from the **two productions of "A Midsummer Night's Dream."**

Olympia Dukakis

TWO SCREENINGS

■ To raise awareness about the fight against heart disease, the first 100 attendees will get a free cholesterol screening when Touching Hearts spokeswoman **Olympia Dukakis** introduces a screening of the film "Steel Magnolias." *5:30 p.m., free. Equitable Center, 787 Seventh Ave., via B,D,E to Seventh Ave.; (212) 448-4311.*

MEN OVER MATTER

■ Photographer Robert Bailey shows the simple tools and raw determination of laborers dismantling giant ships in **"The Ship-Breaking Yards of Bangladesh"** at St. Francis College. *6 p.m. opening reception, free. 180 Remsen St., via 2,3,4,5,M,N, R to Court St./Borough Hall; (718) 489-5272.*

LEN[illegible]OES TECHNO

■ [illegible] a special guest as vir[illegible]ology pioneer **Jaron** [illegible] a spoken workin[illegible] technology demonstra-

OUTDOOR ORCHESTRA

■ Van Cortlandt Park is the **N.Y. Philharmonic's** venue for tonight's outdoor performance of Gershwin, Stravinsky and Bernstein. *8 p.m., free. Parade Grounds; enter at Broadway and 246th St., via 1,9 to 242nd St.; (212) 875-5709.*

SAN JUAN STARS

■ Puerto Rican trombonist **William Cepeda** and his all-star African Jazz Band play hot Latin rhythms influenced by bebop. *6:30 p.m., free. Pier 54, West Side Highway at 13th St., via L,A,C,E to Eighth Ave./14th St.; (212) 533-7275.*

CHUBB-A-DUB

■ Imposing singer/string slinger **Popa Chubby** sings the hit "Sweet Goddess of Love and Beer" from his album "Booty and the Beast." *7 p.m., free. Battery Park City, Wagner Park, enter River Terrace and Chambers St., via 1,2,3,9 to Chambers St.; (212) 416-5300.*

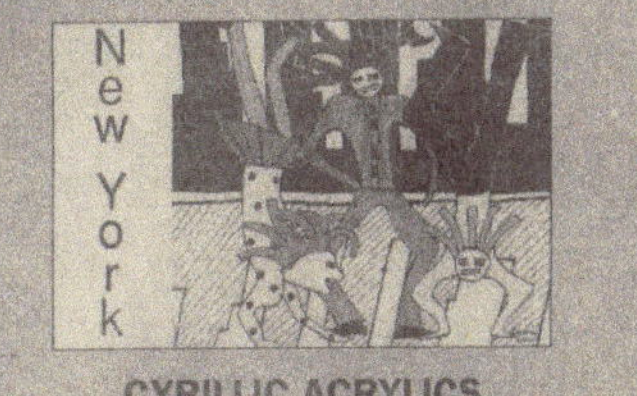

CYRILLIC ACRYLICS

Russian-born artist Nadia Russ shows her bold and fanciful acrylics at Moscow Restaurant. *7 p.m., opening reception, free. 137 E. 55th St., via E,F to Fifth Ave.; (212) 813-1313.*

Battery Park, via 4,5 to Bowling Green; (212) 835-2789.

LITTLE SWINGERS

■ Cast members from the Broadway show "Swing" **teach children about tempos and other basics of dance.** *2 p.m., free with $6 museum admission. Children's Museum of Manhattan, 212 W. 83rd St., via 1,9 to 86th St.; (212) 721-1223.*

Becque in **"South Pacific."** *8 p.m., $20-$25. Fashion Institute of Technology, 227 W. 27th St., via 1,9 to 28th St.; (212) 279-4200.*

LATINA LEADER

■ The struggle of Guatemalan revolutionary leader **Rigoberta Menchu** is portrayed in the docu-

STAR-CROSSED SENIORS

■ **"Mexican Standoff at Fat Squaw Springs"** is a Romeo-and-Juliet story about two romantic seniors fighting off the younger generation trying to separate them. *8 p.m., $12. Vital Theater, 432 W. 42nd St., via A,C,E to 42nd St.; (212) 592-8942.*

FUTURE FILMS

■ **"Cherry Falls"** and its story of a serial killer hunting virgins opens this year's festival celebrating the convergence of film making, the future and technology in sci-fi films. *9 p.m., $5-$12. Chelsea Clearview, 260 W. 23rd St., via C,E to 23rd St.; (212) 691-5519.*

A DIFFERENT STAGE

■ Cast members from **"Riverdance," "Imperfect Chemistry"** and **"Jesus Christ Superstar"** perform songs and dance numbers from their shows. *Noon-2 p.m., free. Bryant Park, 42nd St. and Sixth Ave., via 7,B,D,F,Q to Fifth Ave./42nd St.; (212) 704-1051.*

кроме заработка, имел целый ряд преимуществ: у меня высвободилось дневное время, к тому же я мог бесплатно читать любые газеты и журналы, необходимые мне для постижения и вживания в американскую жизнь. Проработал

тельного фонда. Основная задача фонда — способствовать культурным взаимосвязям двух народов. Мое мнение, Россия и Америка имеют много общего. Это большие по территории страны с пестрым по этническому составу населением.

лерея ориентируется на 10—15 имен, которые будут интересны в основном только специалистам, знатокам и коллекционерам в области искусства. Моя же ориентация — это сотни и тысячи имен

та: я не ориентируюсь на дорогих художников, потому что мой покупатель — не коллекционер и знаток, а простой средний американец. И вот представьте, если такой обыкновенный средний американец,

ционов. Так что, милости просим принять участие в этой, несомненно, интересной акции! Наш телефон для связи: 488-43-63.

Интервью записала
Л. СОЛОВЬЕВА.

КОНОТОП — НЬЮ-ЙОРК

История музыки и вокала знает немало примеров, когда ее знаменательные страницы открывались в ресторанах Парижа и других великих городов мира. Той же чести, судя по всему, удостоился и нью-йоркский ресторан "Латиция", что на Первой авеню, 1352. Но только в другом искусстве — изобразительном. Дело в том, что нижний этаж этого ресторана предоставлен художникам, чьи произведения считаются незаурядными.

Здесь же прошла выставка уроженки Украины, а ныне москвички Надежды МАЛОЛЕТНЕВОЙ.

Трудно подыскать самый точный искусствоведческий термин, который однозначно и адекватно определил бы ее необычную манеру рисовать. Американский журналист Боб Николаидес так охарактеризовал работы Н. Малолетневой, представленные ньюйоркцам в "Хелленик Таймс" в июне 1992 года: "...Ее произведения — работа подсознания, как если бы музыка выражалась в линиях и цвете...".

Что ж, можно допустить и именно такое понимание полотен Надежды. Действительно, только интуитивно, подсознательно, вопреки законам колористики могут возникнуть такие кричащие, резкие цветосочетания, только подсознательно могут появиться невесть откуда взявшиеся линии и формы.

Можно согласиться с трактовкой американского журналиста еще и потому, что художница, получившая музыкальное образование, вправе использовать слуховые ощущения при создании своих "молчаливых" картин. Впрочем, нужно ли их называть молчаливыми, если при всей статичности композиций их линии вот-вот готовы

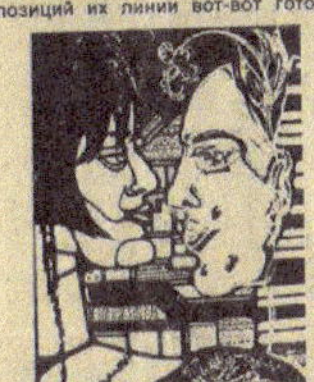

Н. Малолетнева. "Влюбленный".

зазвучать (чаще — ошеломляюще, резко; реже — тихо и мелодично), а краски полотен, откровенно открытые и порой совершенно неожиданные, готовы кричать и резать слух.

В сюжетах Н. Малолетневой нередки человеческие пары: мужчина и женщина. Глаза в глаза — это "Влюбленный". Лицо в лицо — это "Вечерний диссонанс". Персонажи этих работ, возможно, — не только из подсознания, частично они взяты из жизни: вторые — из нью-йоркской; первые могут быть интернациональны. Явно из подсознания "Ветер" с его искаженным человеческим лицом и сильной пластикой. (Справедливости ради замечу, что толкование сюжета не ново в изобразительном искусстве, хотя и нестандартно).

Герои художницы — люди странные. Урбанистический, космический или любой иной антураж, данный вызывающе сочно и броско, лишь подчеркивает человеческую сущность, какой ее видит сегодня художница, — угловатой, контрастной, иногда отталкивающей. Даже клоуны у нее достаточно мрачны ("Клоуны"). Ее "Женский портрет" не притягивает, но привлекает — неожиданными красками и пластикой.

Кажется, художница даже не пробует овладеть пространством: ей хватает и плоскости. "Даунтаунские персонажи" — наркоманы и проститутки, — обитающие в целом городе, спокойно "уживаются" в среде одного прямоугольника. (Не потому ли, что среда эта агрессивна не только к себе самой, но и зрителю?)

Лица, лица... "Мыслитель", "Семья", "Двойной метафизический портрет", "Город в яблоке и лица". Композиционно эти работы построены довольно просто, однако никакого однообразия не ощущается. Хотя постоянно подтверждается однажды созревшая мысль: герои художницы — не добрые гении, а обыкновенные (чаще злые) люди. Нередко — с их страстями и пороками. Сколько же их — таких — повстречала Надежда в своей жизни, чтобы так недобро-честно их показать другим, чтобы хотя бы они не ошибались!..

Родилась Надя 13 декабря 1959 года в небольшом и живописном украинском городе Конотопе, здесь же прошло ее детство. Училась в Курске и Москве.

В конце 80-х годов она создает свои ранние графические работы, пишет гуашью на холсте. Ее работы той поры — их диалог с создательницей. Они вмещают эмоции художницы, состояние человека, чья нервная система еще не вполне готова поделиться самым дорогим ни с кем и ни с чем другим, кроме натянутого на подрамник полотна. И только ему доверяла Надя самое сокровенное — мысли и чувства. Будущей злости было еще немного.

А потом пришло сознание, что свои переживания и боль, переданные холстам, можно сделать достоянием даже совершенно чужих глаз, потому что краски говорили не только о личном, но и о творящихся общественных процессах, о людских судьбах.

Довелось Надежде иллюстрировать рассказы Агаты Кристи, Сахо Сасадзава, получался жанр карикатуры (может быть, от нее — эта жестокость в лицах?).

Выставлялась в групповых выставках в московском Манеже (1990), на Малой Грузинской улице (1991), в Центральном Доме художника (1991). Первую персональную выставку провела в Нью-Йорке (1992). На следующий год выполняла заказ американской фирмы SINGER PATTERN CO., INC.

Пять московских галерей представляли работы Надежды Малолетневой. Есть они в частных коллекциях в России и за рубежом.

Оригинальность творческого почерка художницы ищет развития и признания. И не знаю, стоит ли ей желать избавляться от излишней жесткости в отношении героев. Как знать, вдруг она тогда перестанет быть самой собой.

Игорь ПЕЧКИН

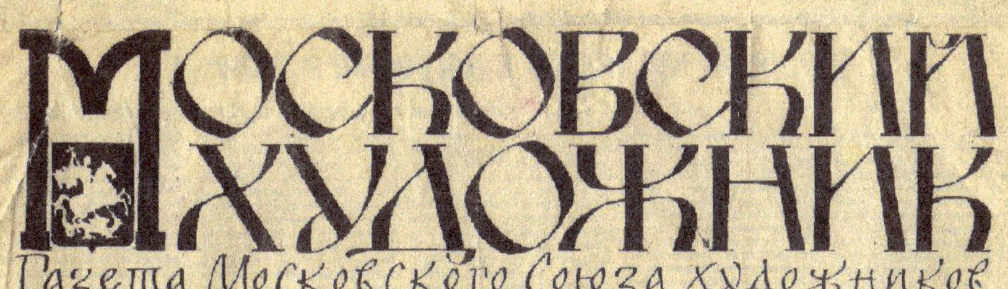

Год издания — 37-й | № 34 (1470) | 20 августа 1993 г. | Цена свободная.

К 100-летию МСХ

Московский Союз

Local News

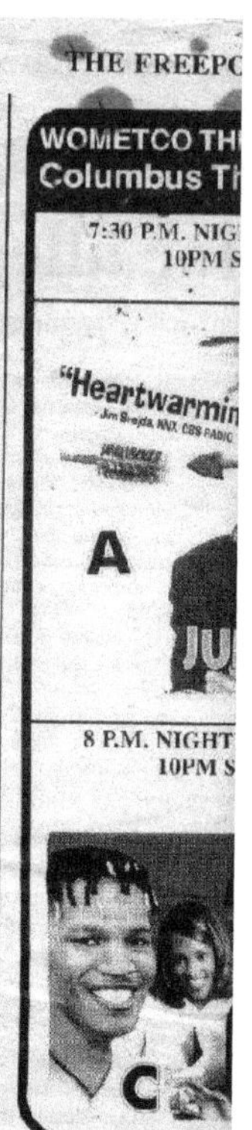

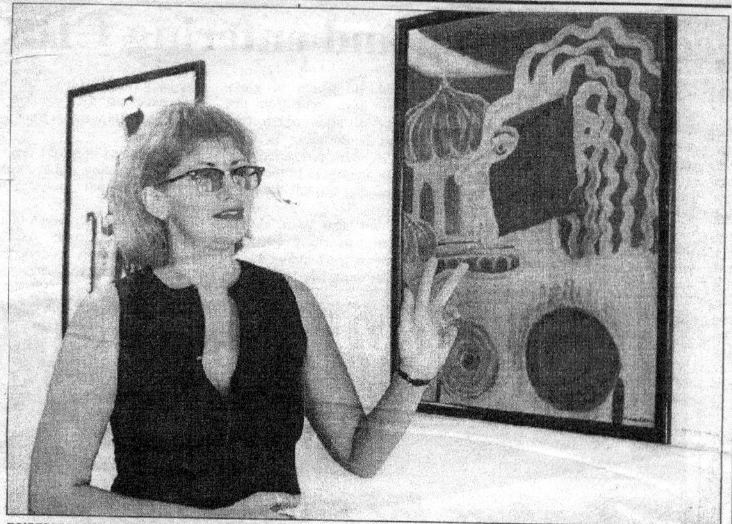

RUSSIAN ART - Nadia is seen describing the concept of one of her Russian inspired paintings which she has titled "Russian Brest Canser." She likened Russia's communistic view to breast cancer, which is an international epidemic. The woman in the painting had her right breast amputated as a result of the cancer which revealed the Russian Crest.
(Photo by Tim Aylen)

Russian artist is very impressed with Bahamas

By JERMAINE SAUNDERS
Freeport News Reporter

Well-traveled Russian Artist Nadia Malolетneva is very impressed with what she has seen and experienced here in The Bahamas and says she will probably reside here one day.

The artist, who currently has an exhibit at the Freeport Art Centre on Queen's Highway, said the atmosphere in The Bahamas gives her something to think about which she can incorporate into her artwork.

"Whereas in Russia," she said, "I am bored with the things I see everyday: people's struggles."

"Here politics is fun. In Russia politics is blood. I am a woman, and I am tired of seeing blood," Nadia added, as she sought to compare the Communist conditions of the Soviet Union to The Bahamas' political democracy.

Nadia said her mentality is a little bit different than the Russian mentality. "I don't think too much about money. I don't want to make too much money, I prefer a simpler life."

Asked when was the first time she discovered her artistic talents, Nadia replied: "When I was a child everybody said: 'you are very talented', why don't you learn art? Nadia recalled. "I started to do it a little better when I became an adult."

Commenting on her change in perception given an entirely different atmosphere here in the Bahamas as opposed to that of Russia where she is a native, Nadia said a different impression can be had depending on the environment she finds herself in.

"When in Russia, I show problems Russians have. When in The Bahamas I will portray Bahamian problems," she noted facetiously.

Also a journalist, Nadia said she started by interviewing

(Continued on Page 6)

The district manager said the need arises.

Russian artist is impressed

(From Page 5)

Russian Congressmen during the time when they were trying to establish a democracy. She continued with her writing, and publishing a number of books. Since then she has stuck with producing art.

"I like to paint faces," Nadia revealed. "Because a face of a person is like a looking glass of the soul. By looking at the face it is possible to find out everything about a person, almost everything."

Said Nadia: "The face reflects intellect, mood, and feelings. By means of the face you can get to know human essence."

On appreciation, Nadia said quite a bit of patrons "who do not like to think" have a problem understanding her type of work. Instead, she added, they would rather see beautiful pictures of trees, clouds and other calming, picturesque scenes.

"My art is puzzling someone said," she recollected. "Someone would need to be somewhat of an intellect to appreciate my art."

The best of everything is created when the mind is in a state of absolute liberation, when there is no chaining limits to destroy movement of thought, the Russian artist told **The Freeport News** yesterday.

"I think art is best done when a person is experienced. If you paint nature you don't need experience, but if you do something from your mind you must have experience. It is only necessary to find the key to yourself and thereafter everything depends on one's capability for work..." is the motto Nadia patterns her art life by.

Nadia, during her many art exhibitions, has gained favour from various art connoisseurs including Bob Nicolaides of the Hellenic Times in New York who said: "Nadia's artwork is that of subconscious, that is, music exposed in lines and colour."

In addition to a local exhibition to be held until April 12, at the Freeport Art Centre on Queen's Highway beginning at 10:00 a.m., Nadia has hosted art shows from 1989 to the present in numerous art galleries in her native land, Russia, and New York.

She now adds The Bahamas to her itinerary.

NeoPopRealism STARZ

PRESENTS:

Erotica as a High Artistic Aspiration

Andrzej Michael Kawasaki (USA), **Sigmund Abeles** (USA), **Pete Herzfeld** (USA), **Joseph Borzotta** (USA), **Milan Kuzica** (Czech Republic), **Megh** (USA), **Jacob El Hanani** (USA), **Paolo Scalera** (UK), **Shana Calano** (USA), **R. Gopakumar** (India/Bahrain), **Don McCormack** (USA), **Matthew Goglianese** (USA), **Charles Seligman** (USA), **Leanne Maloney** (USA), **Terry Brown** (USA), **Frederique Krzis-Lorent** (France), **David DeRosa** (USA), **Julie Donec** (Canada), **Mark Schieferstein** (USA), **Mohammed Yasin Saddique** (UK), **Viliam Sulik** (Slovakia), **Stefan Havadi-Nagy** (Germany)

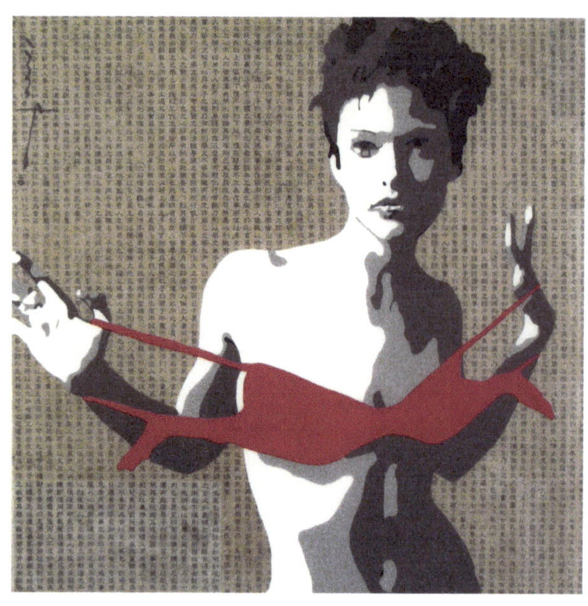

Andrzej Mchael Kawasaki (USA), *Love and Lust*, Acrylic, mixed media and resin on birch panel, 24"x24"

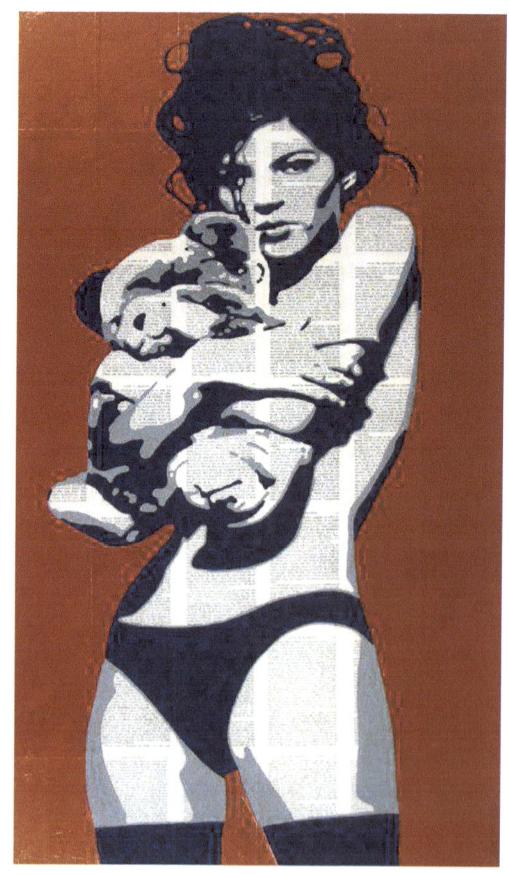

Andrzej Michael Kawasaki (USA), *Tao of Poh*, acrylic, mixed media and resin on birch panel, 24"x48"

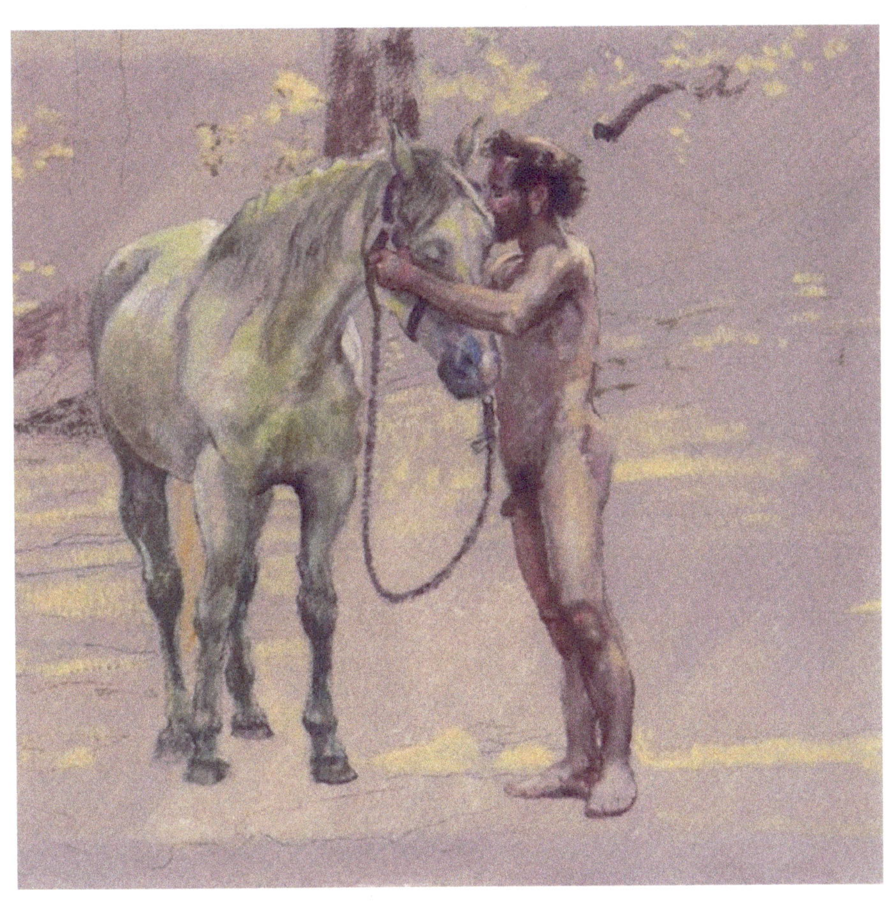

Sigmund Abeles (USA), *6 Feet Above Ground*

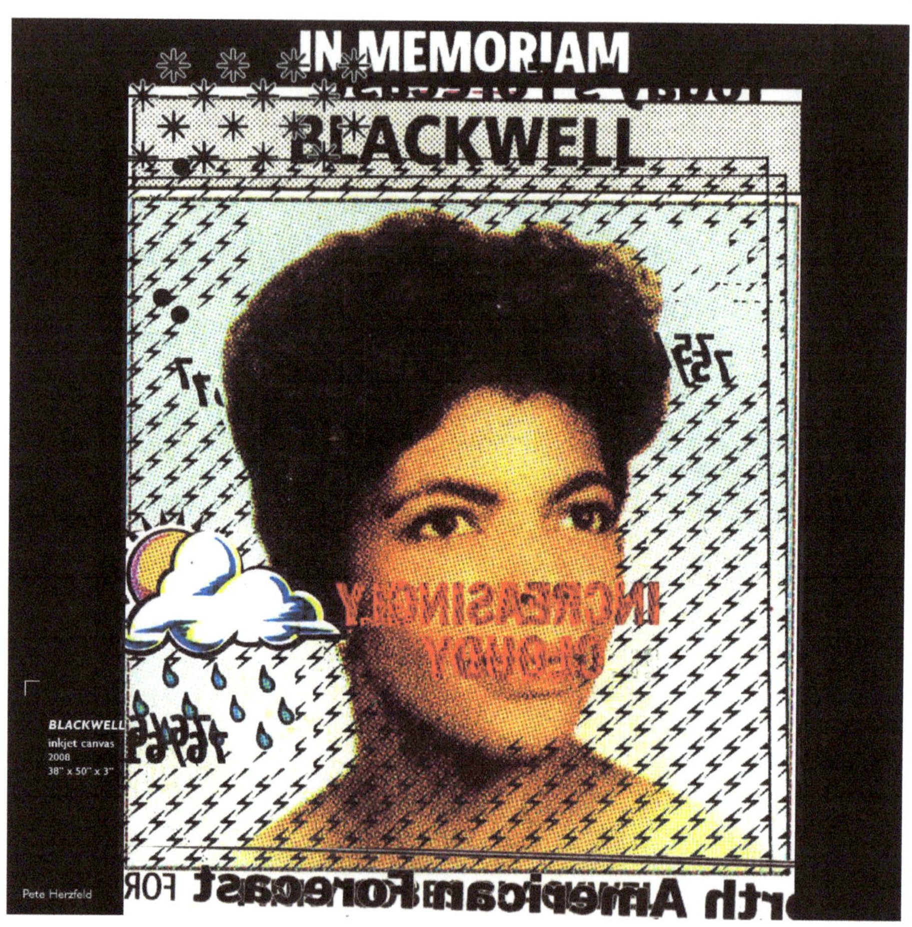

Pete Herzfeld (USA), *Blackwell*, 50"x40"x3"

EROTICA AS A HIGH ARTISTIC ASPIRATION

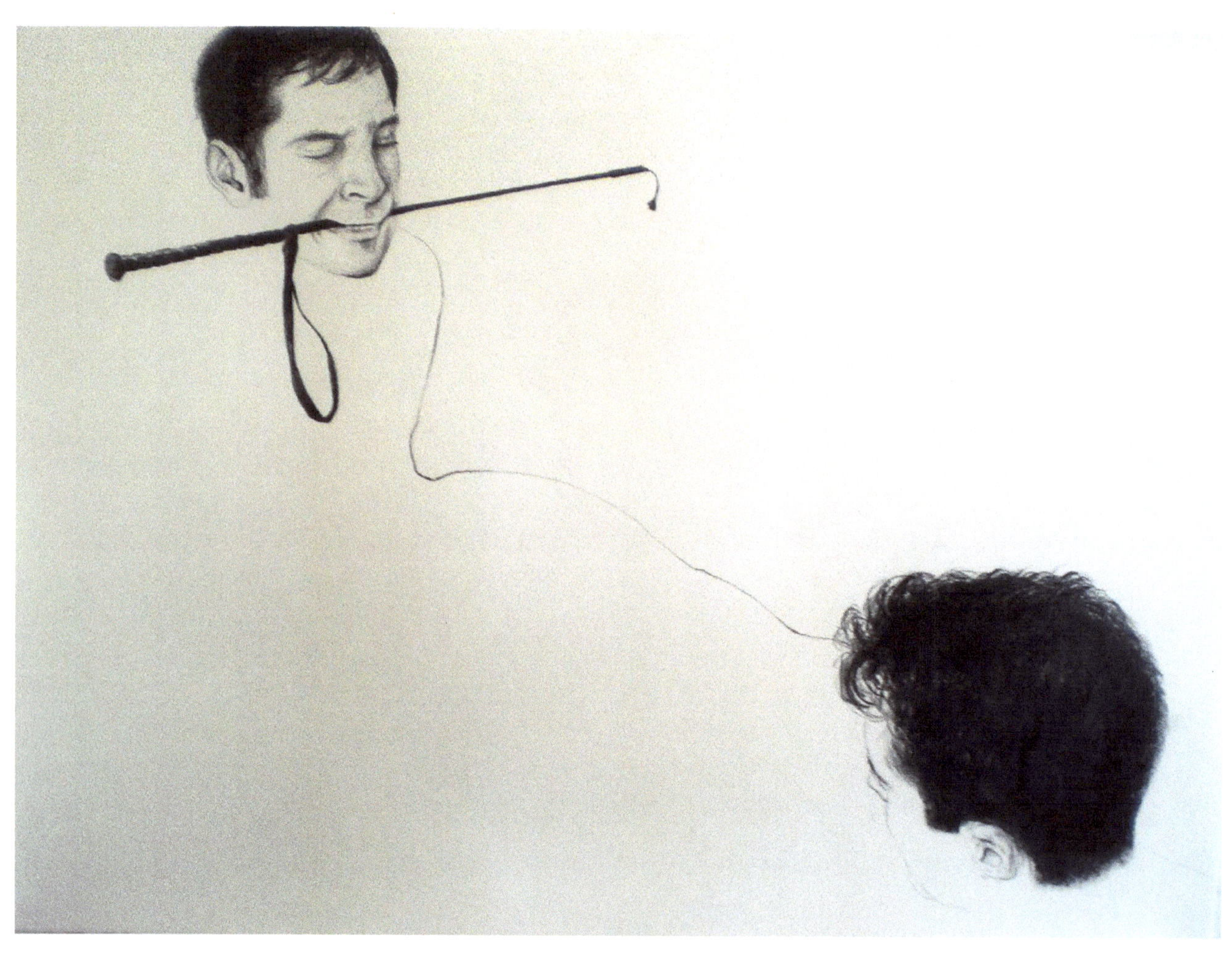

Joseph Borzotta USA), *Riding Crop-2 Guys,1 Girl*, Graphite on paper, 30"x20"

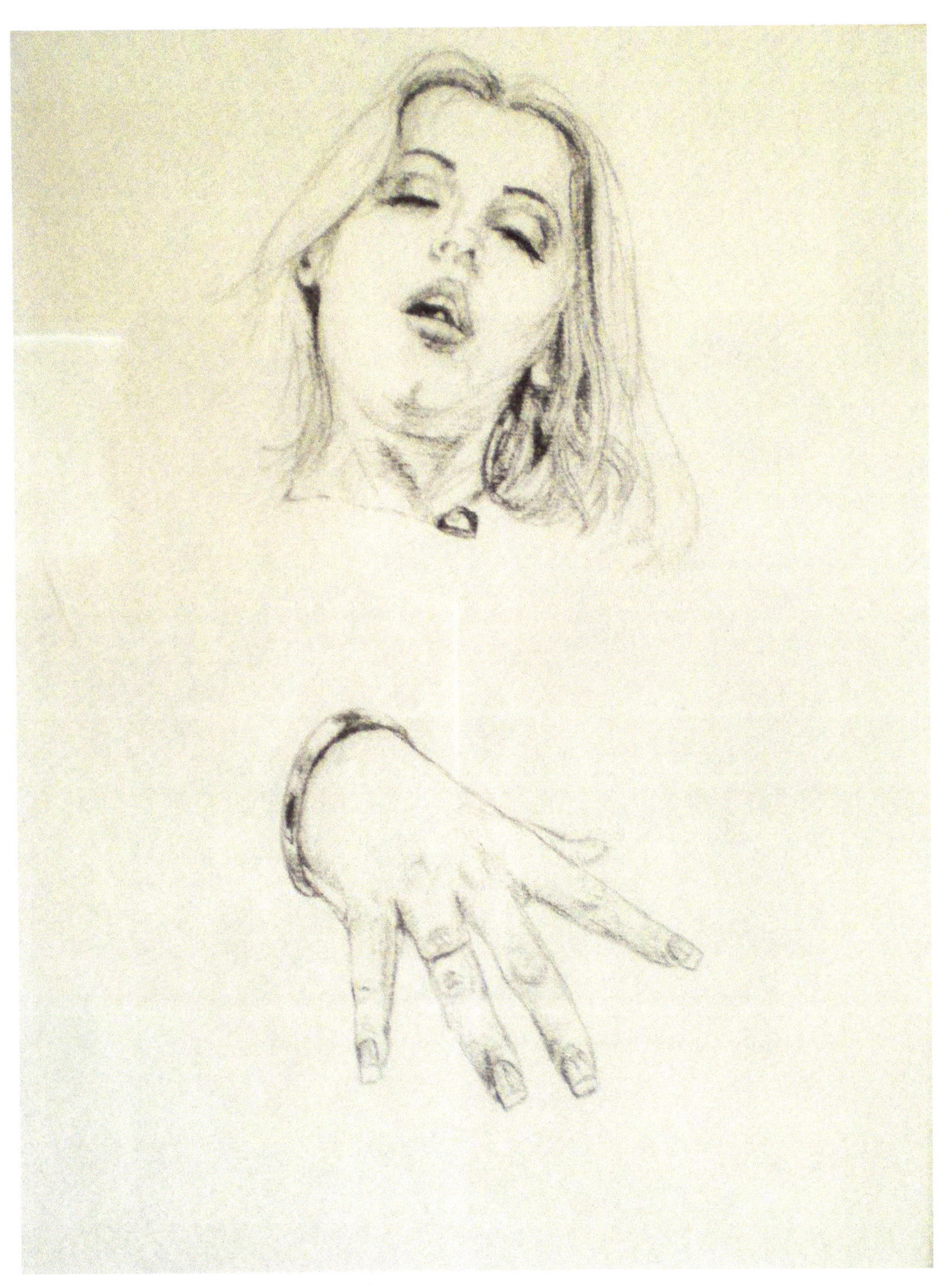

Joseph Borzotta (USA), *Girl-Solo*, graphite on paper, 9"x12"

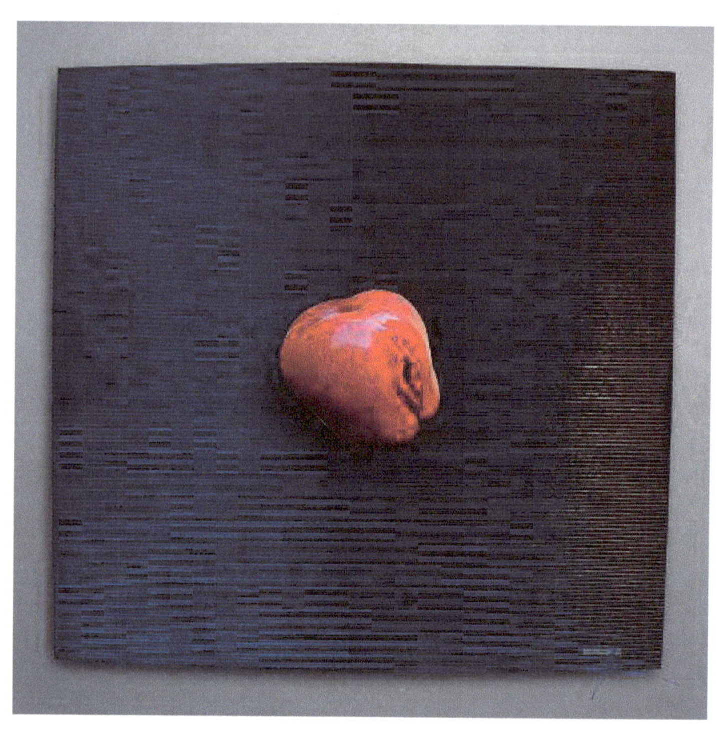

Milan Kuzica (Czech Republic), *Ordinary Seed,* mixed media, 14,9"x14,9"x0,4"

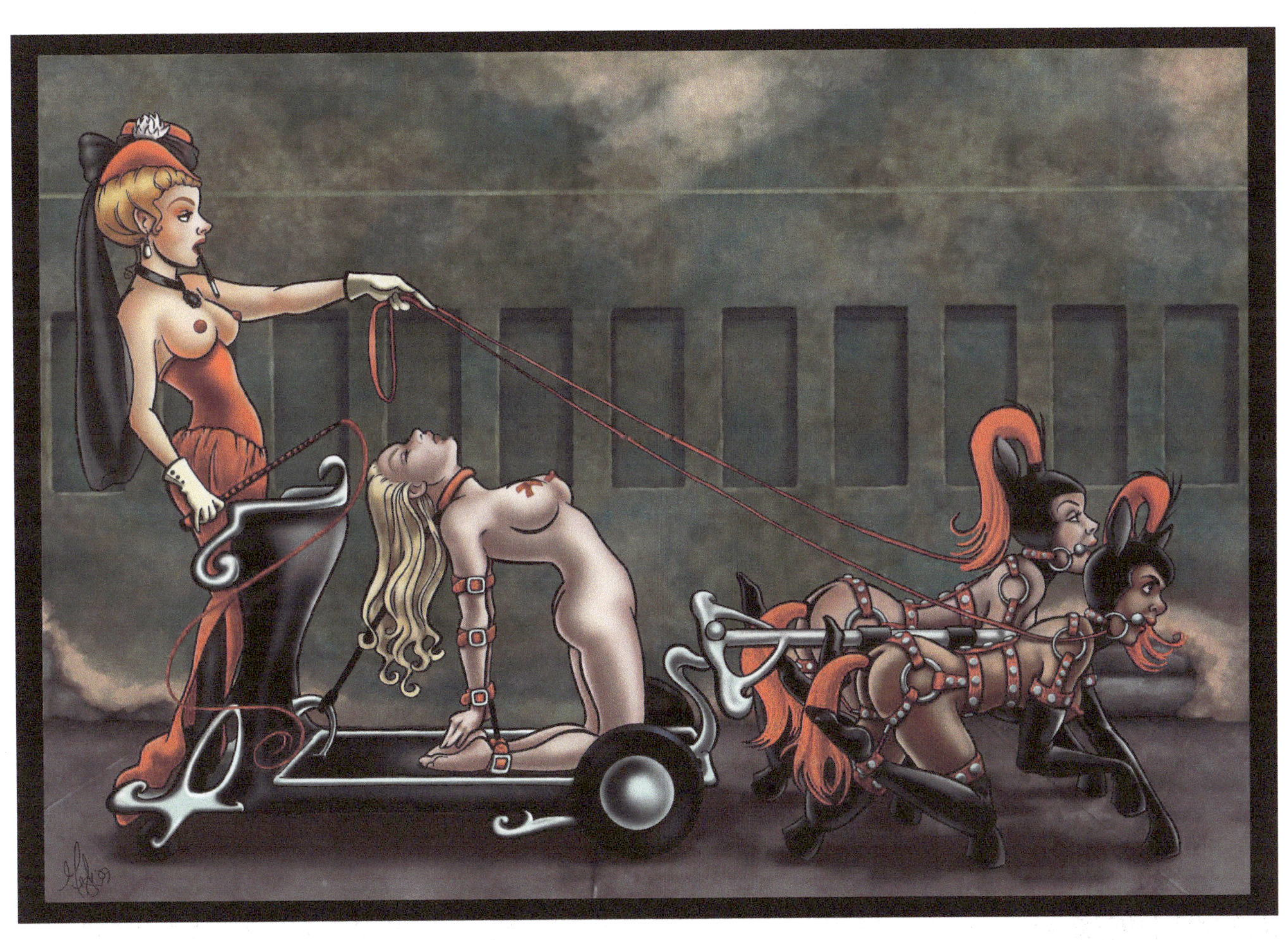

Meghan Vaughan (Megh) (USA), *Special Delivery*, mixed media, 12"x17"

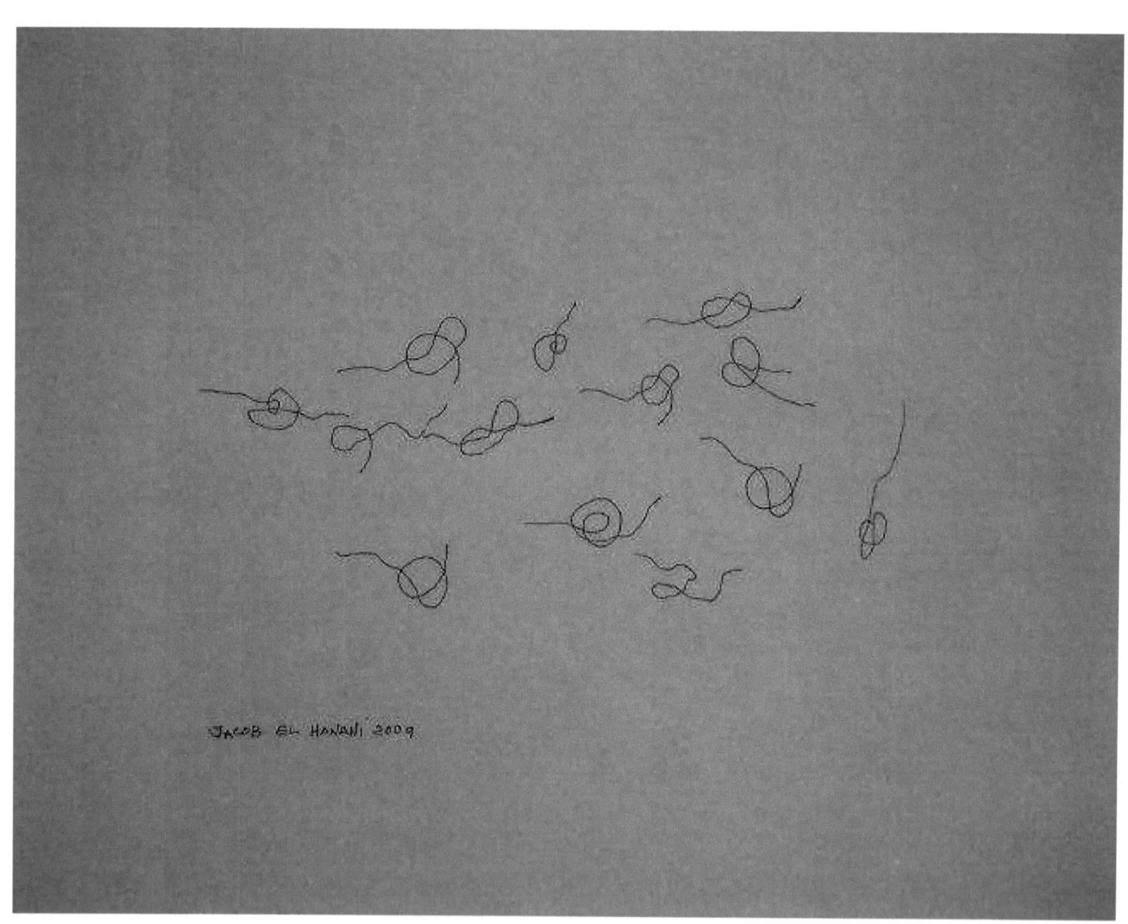

Jacob El Hanani (USA), *Untitled*, Ink drawing, 7"x9"

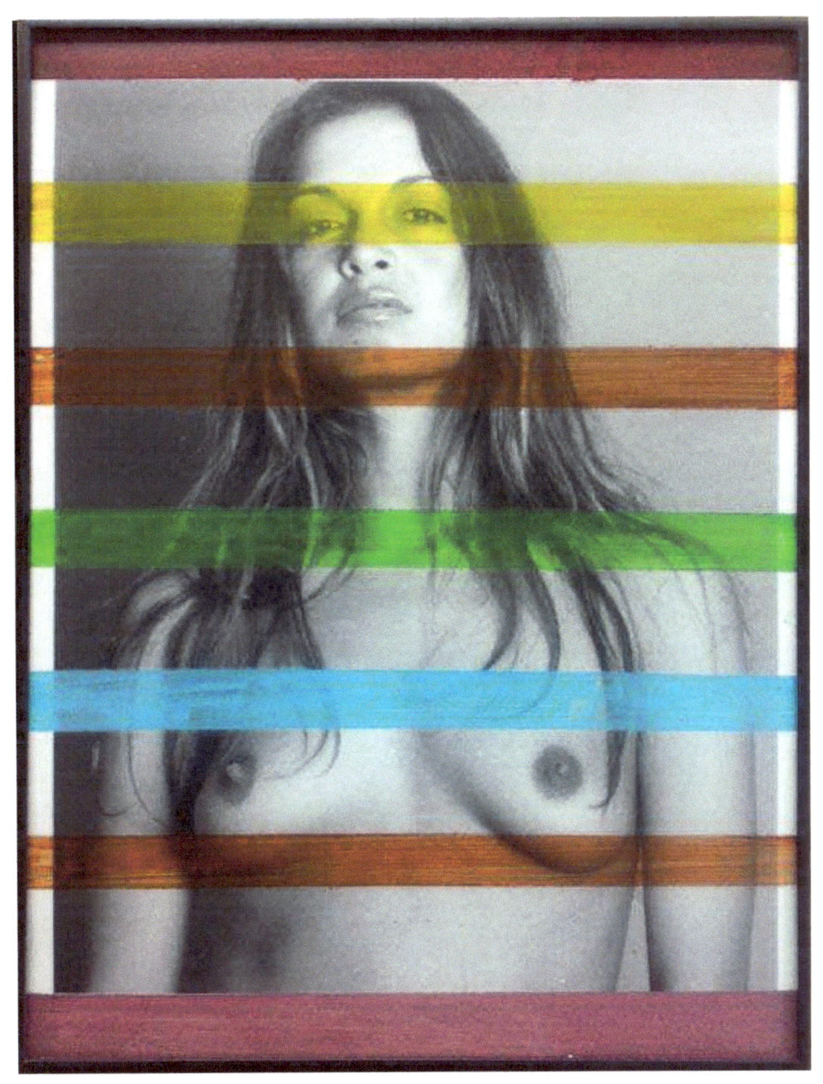

Paolo Scalera (UK), *Roberta*, photography, 40cmx50cm

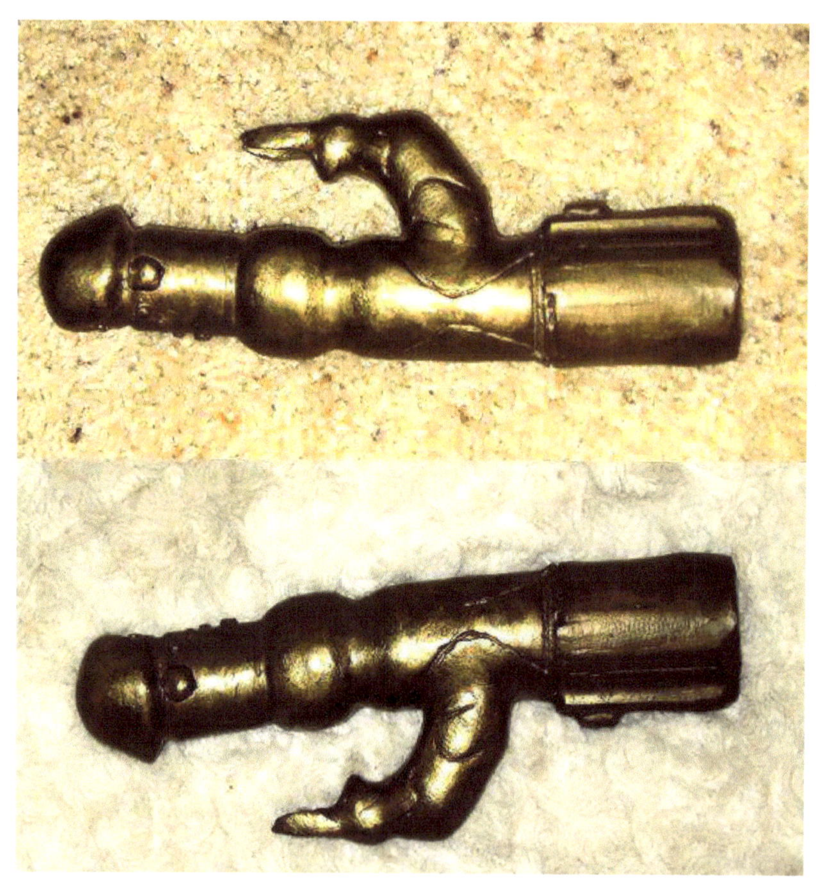

Shana Calano (USA) *Rabbit*, bronze, 9"x3"

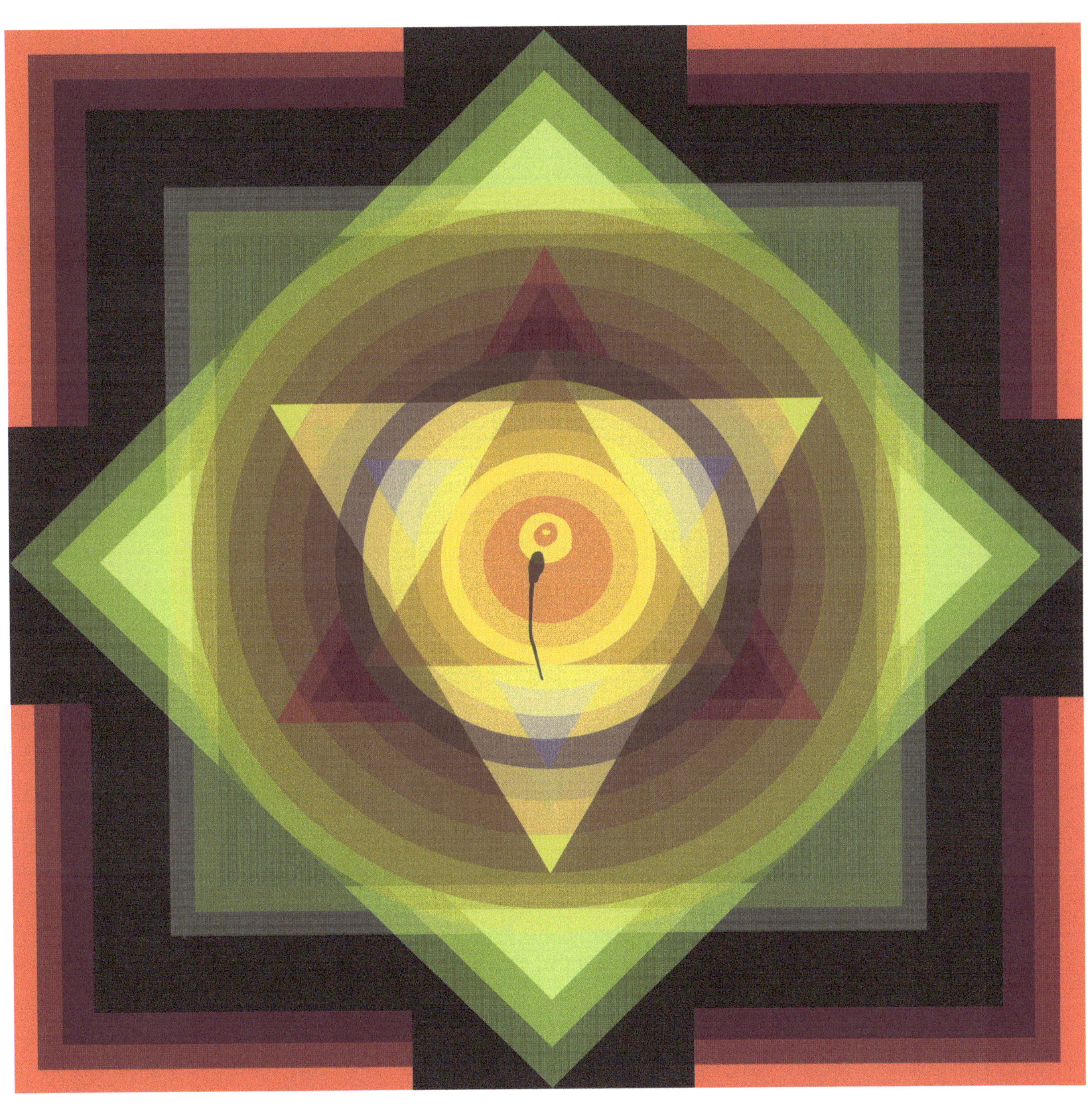

R. Gopakumar (India/Bahrain), *Cognition-Libido*, digital print, 80cmx80cm

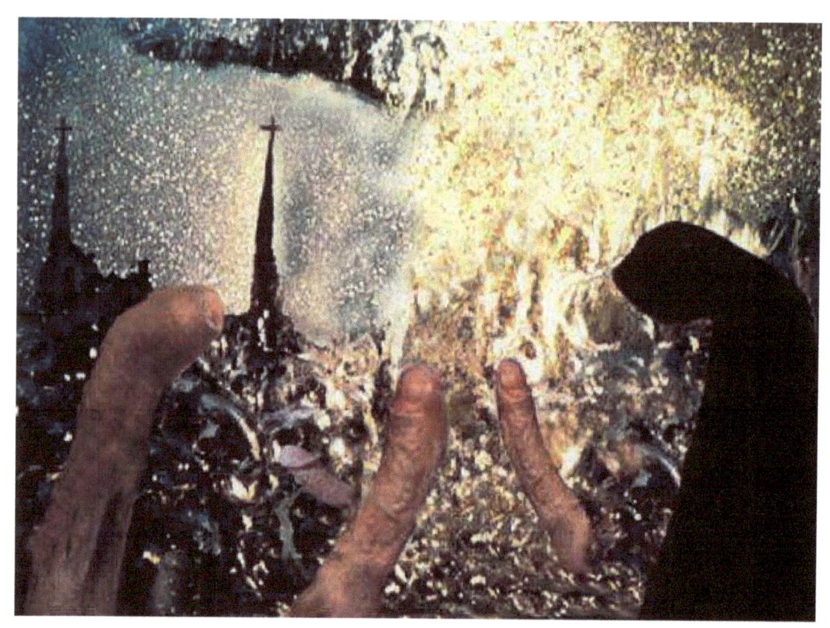

Don Marphy (USA), *Salvation is Difficult*, computer art, ink jet print, 13"x19"

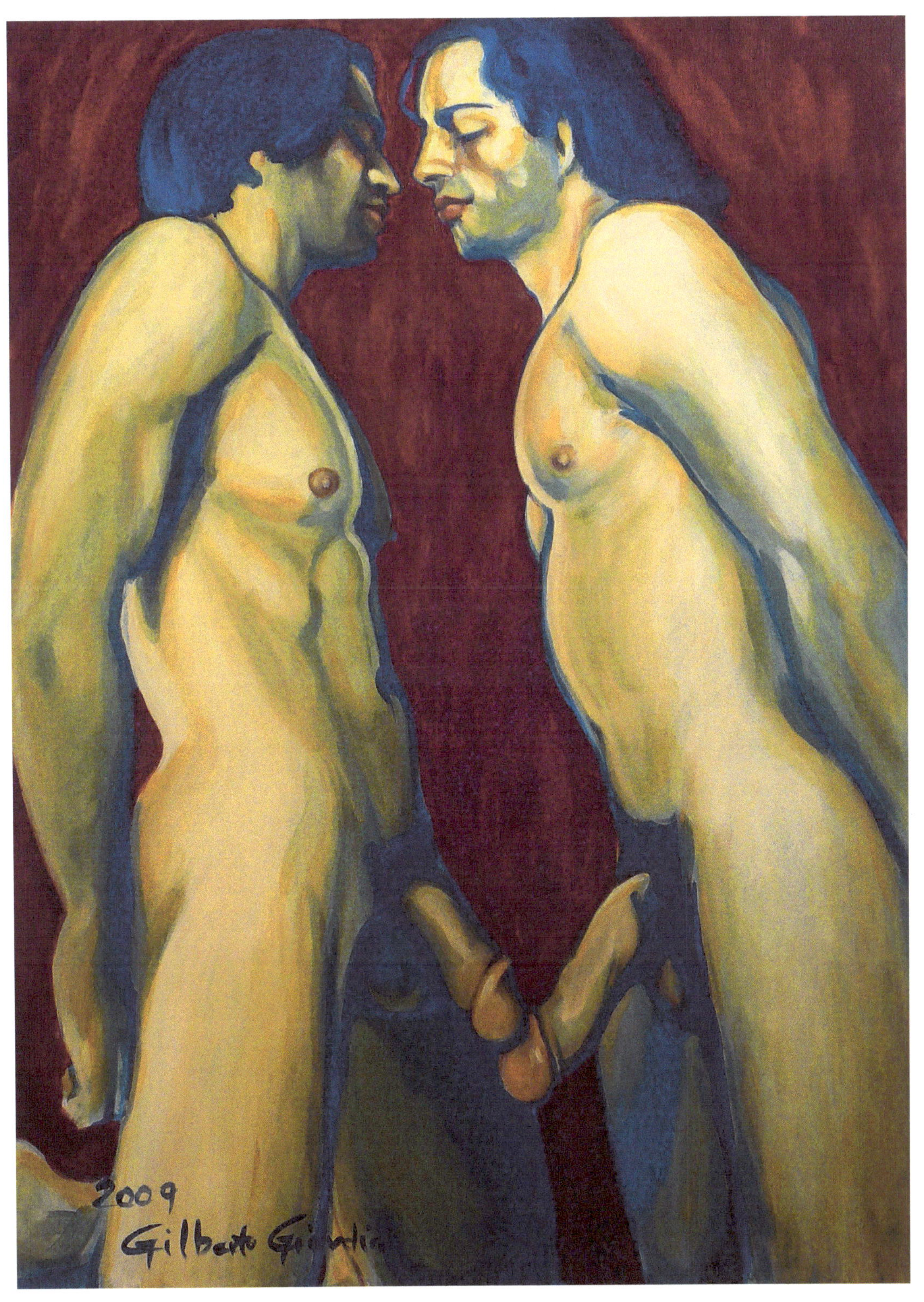

Gilberto Giardini (Germany), *High Potential,* acrylic on canvas, 70cmx100cm

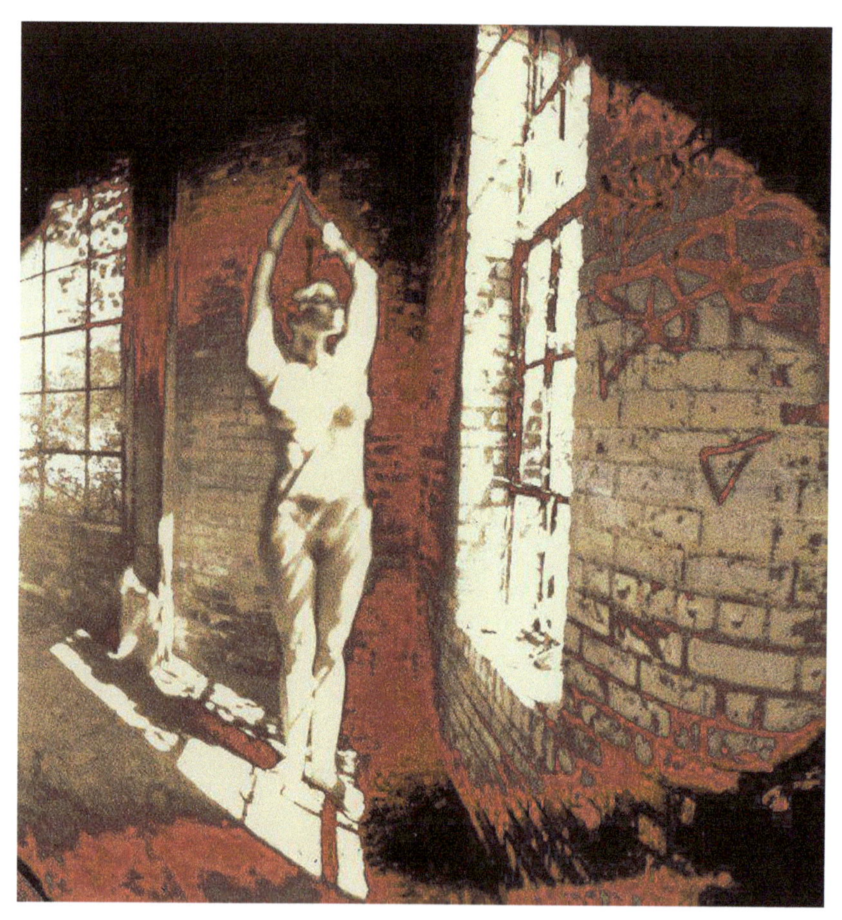

Don McCormack (USA), *Tracy-5-20-03-44BA*, photography, 22.5"x20"

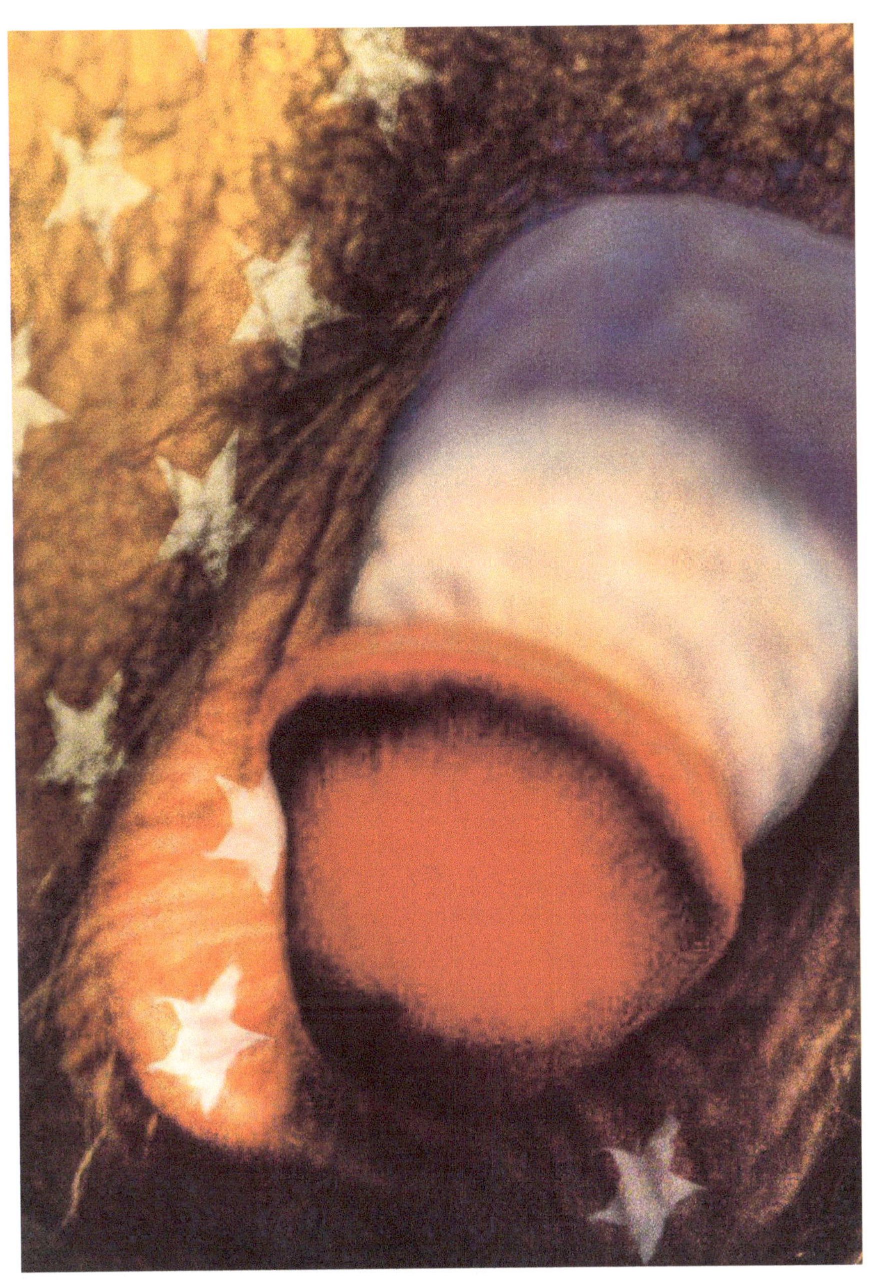

Matthew Coglianese (USA), *The American Wang*, photography/digital, 18"x 24"

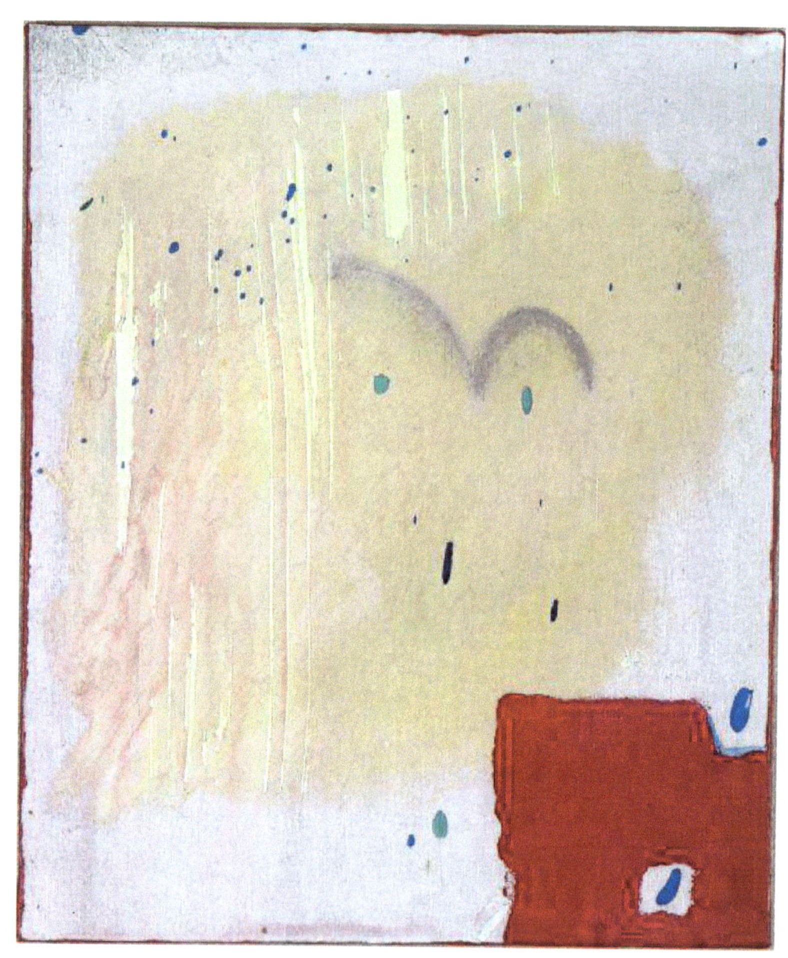

Charles Seligman II (USA), *Hoot,* acrylic/canvas. 16"x20"

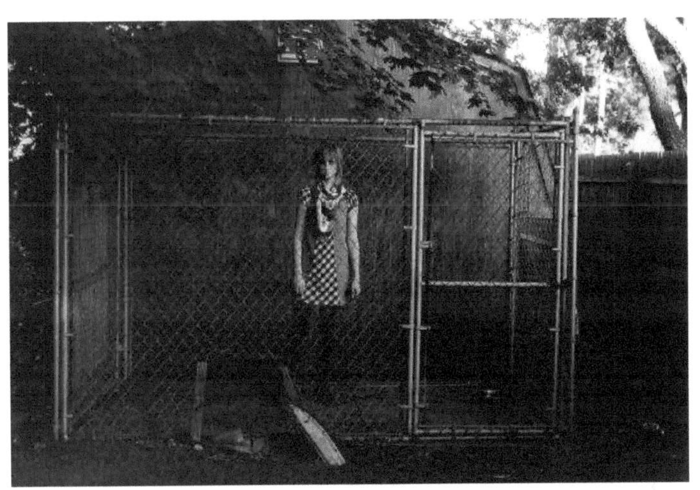

Leanne Maloney (USA), *Chainlinked*, photography, 11"x14"

21st century art

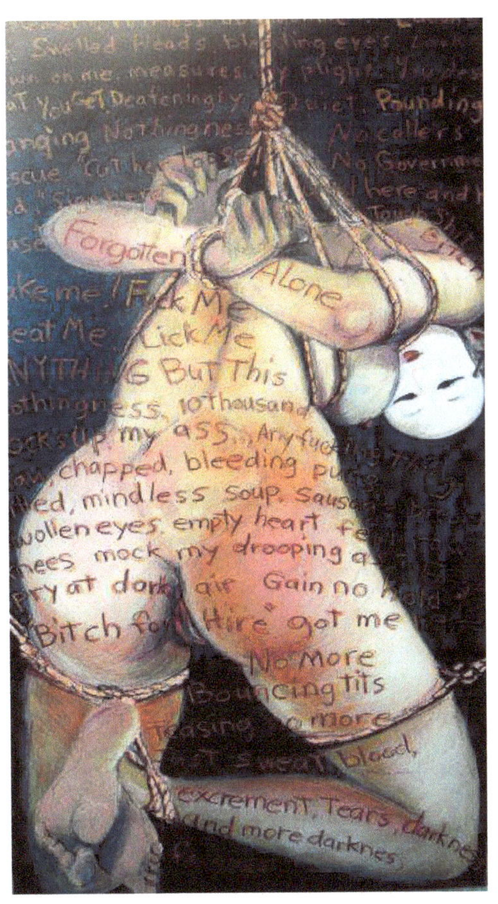

Terry Brown (USA), *Unintended Consequence*, oil and charcoal, 24"x48"

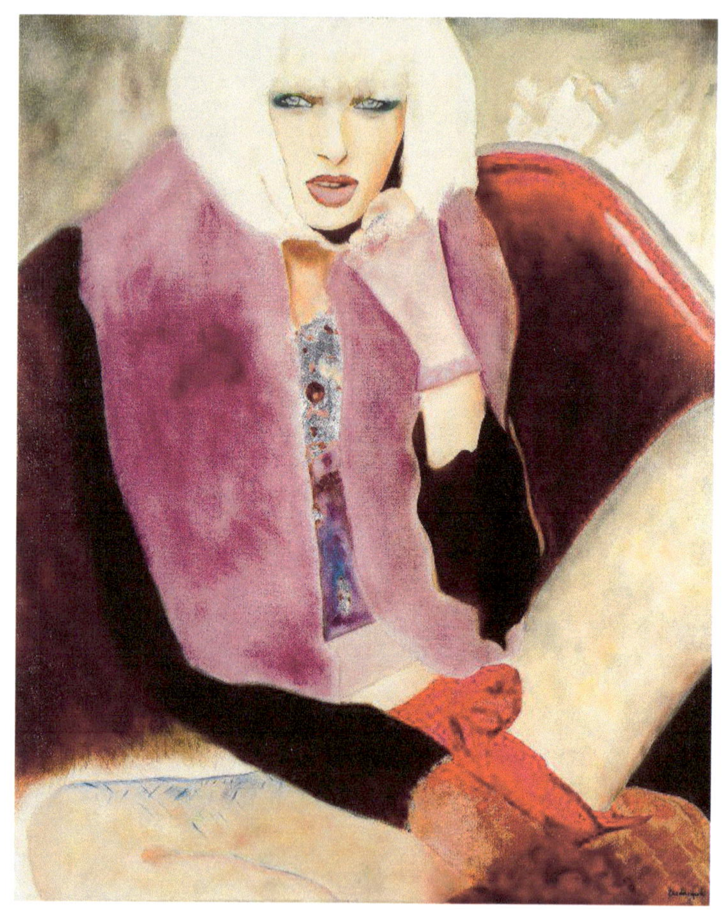

Frederique Krzis-Lorent (France), *Icon*, oil/canvas, 73cmx92cm

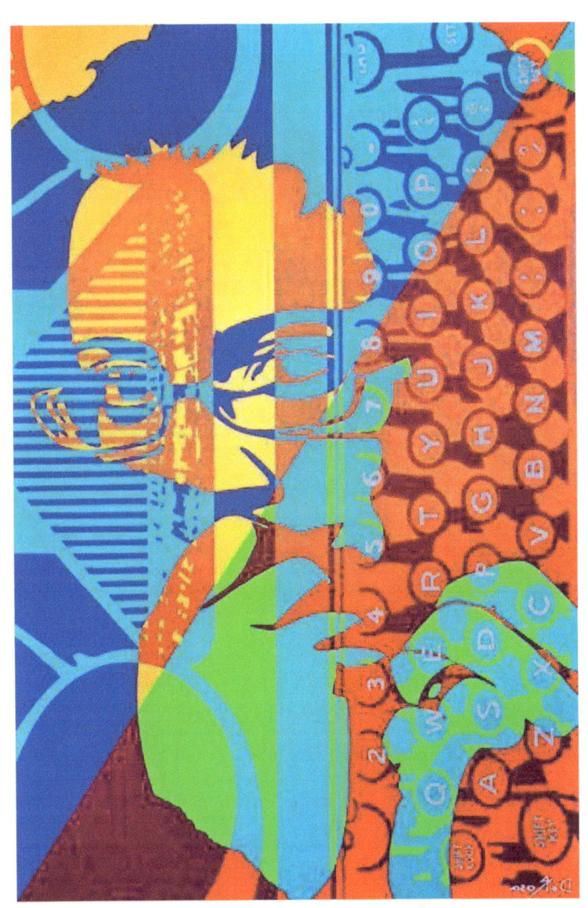

David DeRosa (USA), *The Venus of Typography*, acrylic on wood panel, 22.25"x36"

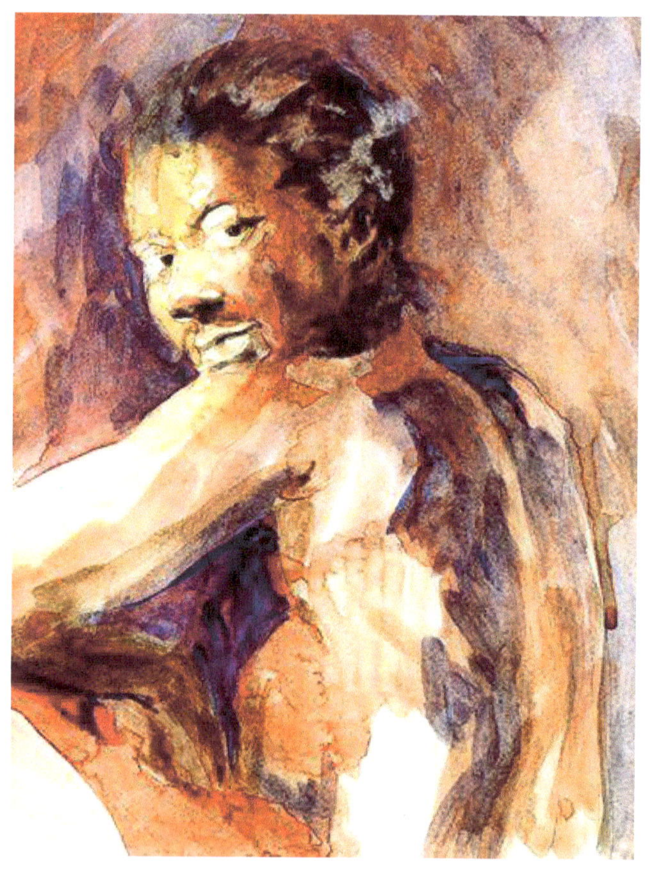

Julie Donec (Canada), *Study for A Fallen Angel*, watercolor on board, 14"x11.5"

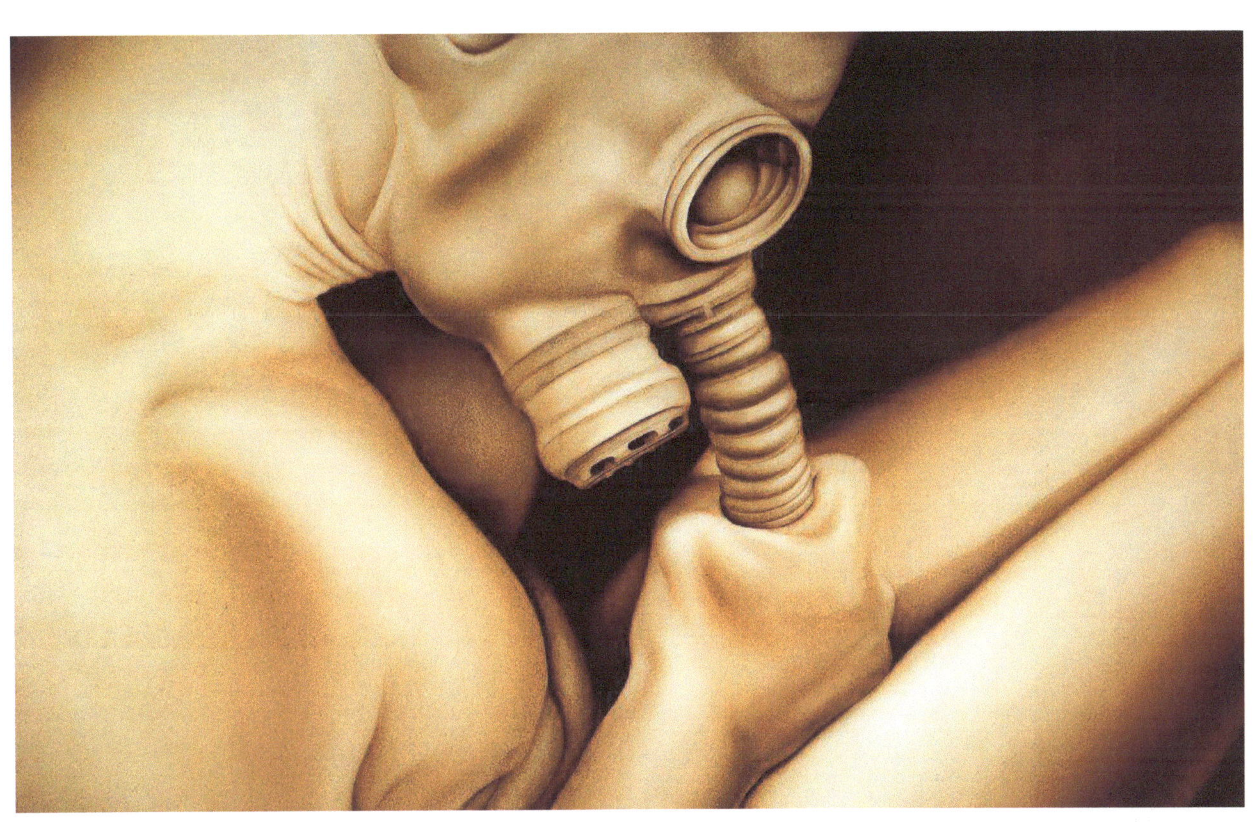

Mark Schieferstein (USA), *Nozzle*, oil, 47.875"x30"

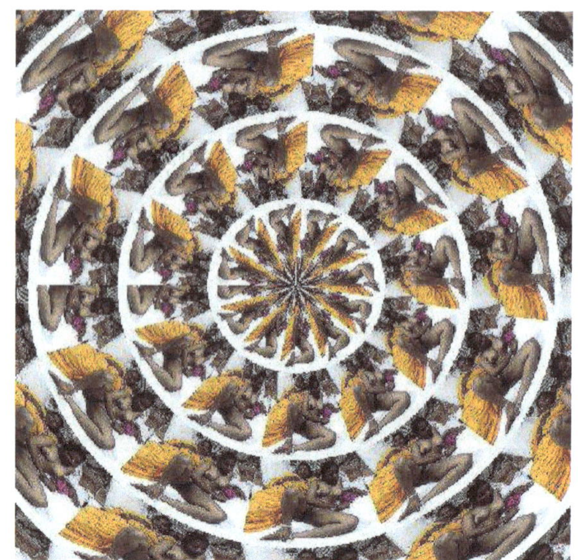

Mohammed Yasin Saddique (UK), *Nude Indian Woman,* digital photo on foam board

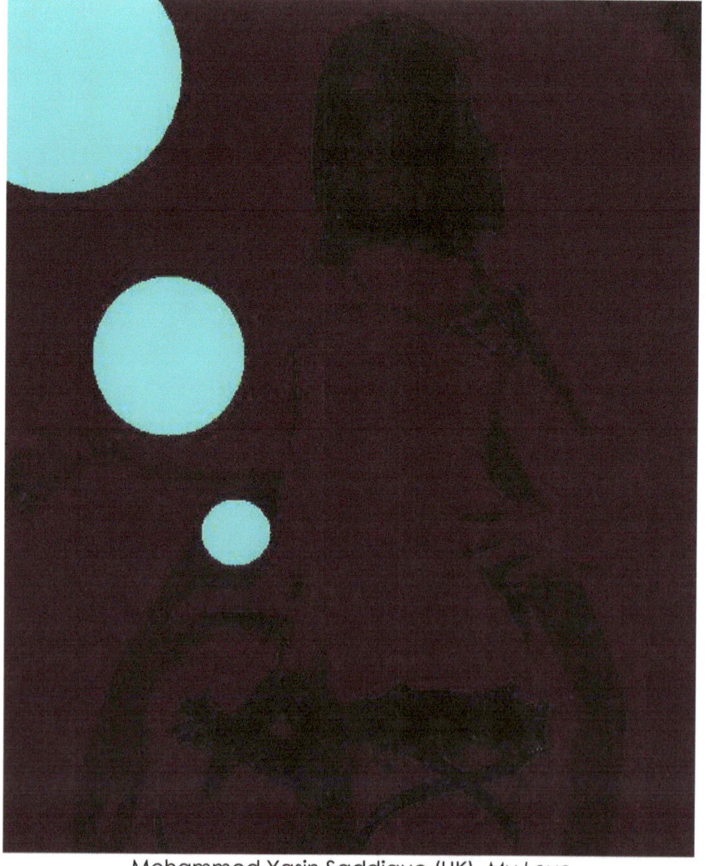

Mohammed Yasin Saddique (UK), *My Love,* digital photo on foam board

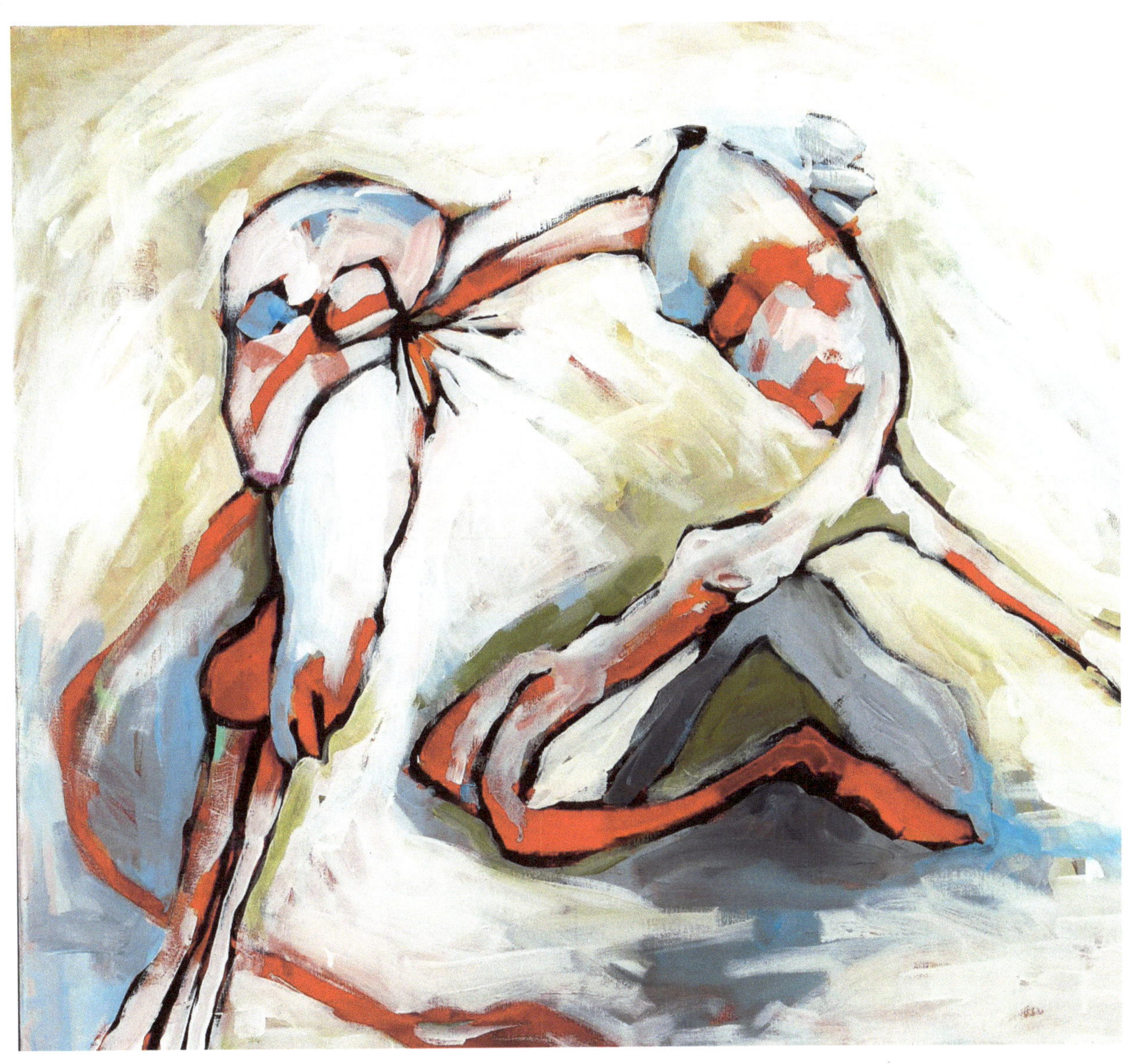

Viliam Sulik (Slovakia), *Choicy Lovers,* acrylic/banvas, 82cmx92cm

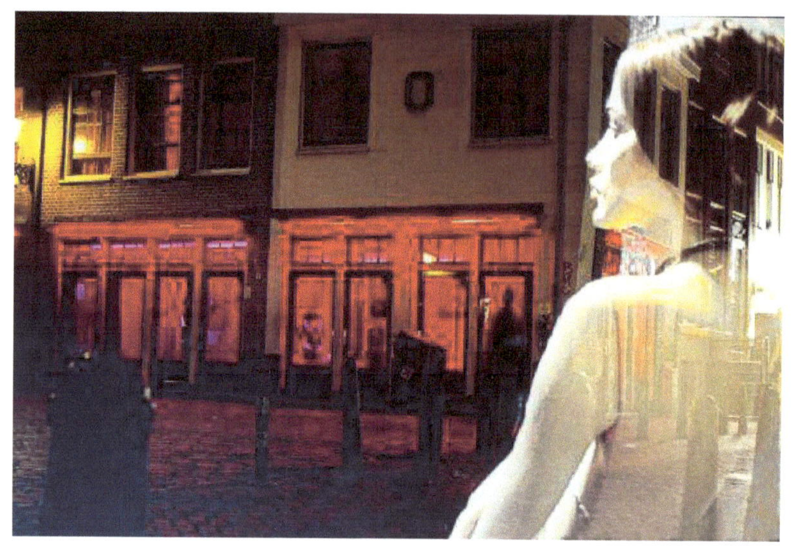

Stefan Havadi-Nagy (Germany), *Toys*, photograph, 70cmx55cm

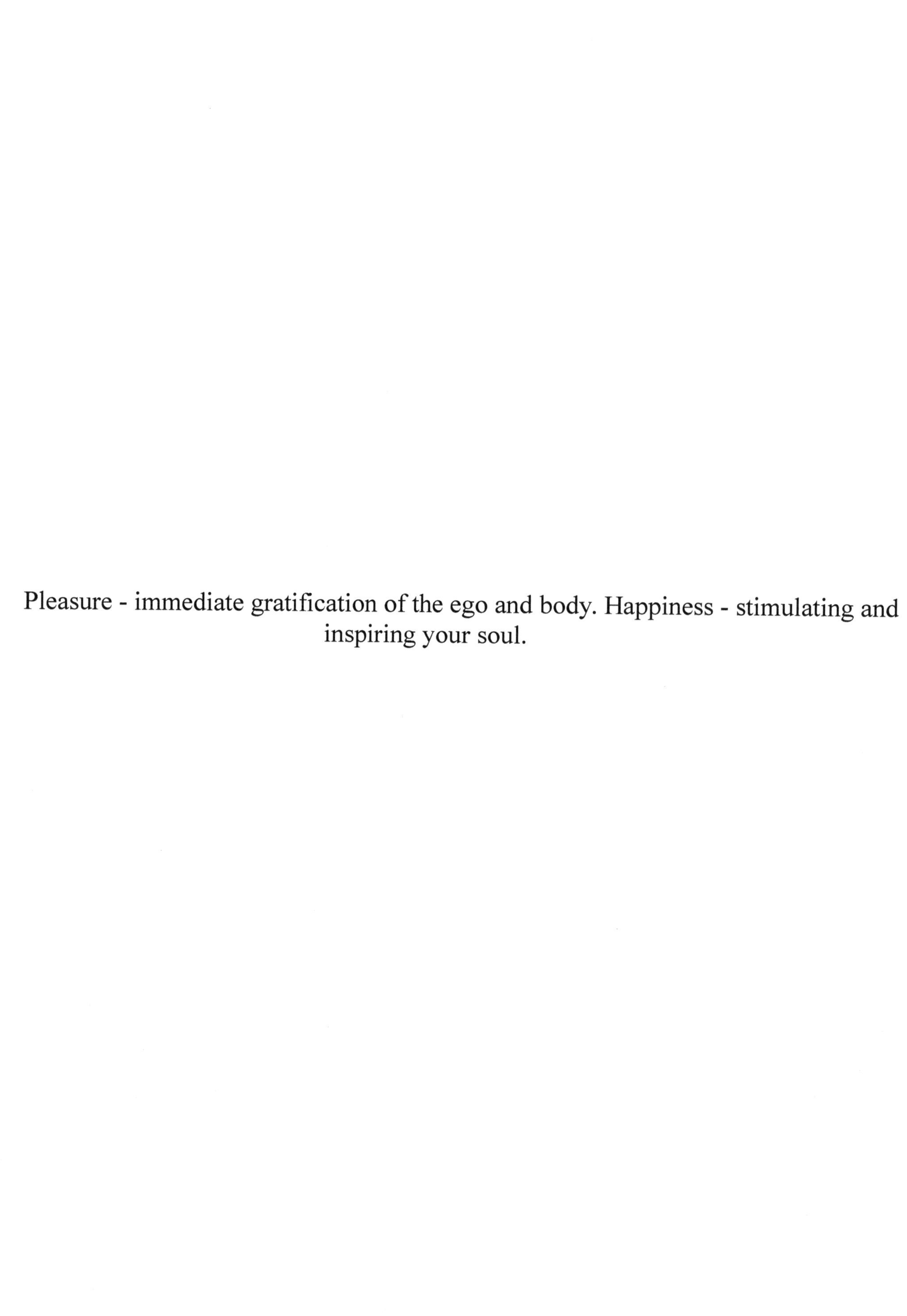

Pleasure - immediate gratification of the ego and body. Happiness - stimulating and inspiring your soul.

Artists' Thoughts

Andrzej Michael Karwaski: "Love and Lust is a representation of human basic instincts of temptation." (page 28)

Sigmund Abeles. "6 Feet Above Ground". (Page 29)

Pete Herzfeld. "Blackwell: My inkjet "paintings " attempt to illustrate the socio-politico tension generated by death. When we die, we live in our wake a trial of artifacts and places that we have shaped, constructed and designed. I am particularly interested in the power of places and artifacts to tell the stories of people who may passed through. . . (Page 30)

Joseph Borzotta. "Riding Crop: Images for X-rating products are often censored with the infamous black lines or dots over the "naughty bits" leaving an image that is either odd, comedic, as equally risqué as the original image - or all of the above. I began to replicate images from adult magazines in graphite with shapes of color acting as censorship marks, yet becoming decorative and transforming the image. I then left out the shapes of color and began to subtract more information leaving as little as possible yet still retaining some of the original intent of the image. Porn is dehumanizing, so this mineralization of the people into parts and pieces reflects that, yet the faces remind us that these are still human beings. Their expressions are amusing and tragic at the same time. (Page 32-33)

Milan Kuzica. "Ordinary Seed: "The woman you put here with me - she gave me some fruit from the tree, and I ate it." Gen 3.12)" (Page 34)

Maghan Vaughan (Megh). "Special Delivery". (Page 35)

Jacob El Hanani. "Untitled: It could be interpreted as erotica or make viewer to think about erotica." (Page 36)

Paolo Scalera. "Roberta is a simple fashion shot of a Model combined with acrylic painted strips to give more edge to the image." (Page 37)

Shana Calano. "Rabbit was created with multiple purposes (and no, not for my own personal fulfillment). First of all, it is homage to the rabbit vibrator, which is a very popular model of vibrator and was even shown in Sex And The City. Secondly and most importantly, I made this piece to accompany a bizarre story I made up about the world in hundreds of years. Women rule the earth and pray to the great dildo gods that bring them satisfaction. The women in this world light candles and throw coins around the sculpture . . ." (Page 38)

R. Gopakumar. "Cognitive-Libido: I like layers, the sand layers of the desert that forms after the soft wind, the mud layers of the pond after reduction of the water, same way the pieces of the onion and meat are all influenced my paintings patterns. These layers are the basic concept of the universe." (Page 39)

Don W. Murphy. "Salvation is Difficult was finished in 2009." (Page 40)

Gilberto Giardini. "High Potential: this painting captures the excitement and restless anticipation of two men's first sexual encounter." (Page 41)

Dan McCormack. "Tracey-5-20-03-44BA: for over forty years I explore various techniques and processes while photographing the nude as a central theme. In 1998, I began to work with pinhole photography." (Page 42)

Mtthew Coglianese. "The American Wang: HDR photography with some editing in Photoshop. This image was created from a curiosity to shoot HDR photography of a nude model, which was then Americanized by showing off the patriotic colors." (Page 43)

Charles Seligman II. "Hoot". (Page 44)

Leanne Maloney. Chainlinked. (Page 45)

Terry Brown. "Unintended Consequence". (Page 47)

Frederique-Krzis-Lorent. "Icon". (Page 48)

David DeRosa. The Venus of Typography. (Page 50)

Julie Donec. "Much of my work is figurative, and for the last number of years I have explored the themes of duality (light vs. dark nature of man's consciousness), using the allegorical framework of angels and devils. The Study For a Fallen Angel is a watercolor sketch of one of my models; his strong features and an elusive quality he had when he looked over his shoulder serve as the inspiration for the piece." (Page 51)

Mark Schieferstein. "Nozzle: this boy of work exposes the cruelty of intimacy and depicts a vision of darkness. Increasingly erotic and unapologetic, this painting is a means of self-discovery." (Page 52)

Mohammed Yasin Saddique. "My Love" and "Nude Indian Woman". (Page 53)

Viliam Sulik. "Choicy Lovers reflects the intimacy of a man and a woman. In spite of relatively static composition, there's a certain disturbance or unbalance. It's depicting a slight dominance of a man in a libertine sense. . ." (Page 54)

Stefan Havadi-Nagy. "Toy"s. (Page 55)

Also available a book *NeoPopRealism Starz: 21st Century ART, Compendium of New Millennium Contemporary Art, Vol.1* with Nadia Russ' article *NeoPopRealism Evolution* in foreword and artworks from 14 artists from all over the world.

Article 'NeoPopRealism Evolution'

I was working on the subject of *NeoPopRealism* for several years. But only in the new millennium I was ready to present *NeoPopRealism* to the world. *NeoPopRealism* as a style of visual arts combines brightness and simplicity of Pop Art and deep psychological realism, has high energy colors and graphic nature. Word *NeoPopRealism* and concept I created January 4, 2003. *NeoPopRealism* and its cultural expressions are rooted in the art traditions, and are intimately linked to a community sense of identity and self determination. *NeoPopRealism* indicated the essential turning point in the art history. *NeoPopRealism* art possessing artistic qualities of Pop Art and realism.

Invention of *NeoPopRealism* in visual arts is essentially logical extension of the art evolution. It was reserved to 21st century to witness an invention of visual arts—*NeoPopRealism*. It was significant necessity, reflecting new millennium. An invention is seldom a mater of chance. It was a response to a deep, general need, which is at ones intellectual and creative.
NeoPopRealism is a natural extension of evolution:
60th—Andy Warhol and Jasper Johns with Pop Art;
80th—Jeff Koons with his Neo-Pop; at the beginning of the new millennium I manifested *NeoPopRealism* . . .

NeoPopRealism commandments reflect needs of 21 century:
1. Be beautiful;
2. Be creative;
3. Be peace-loving, positive-minded;
4. Do not accept communist philosophy;
5. Be free-spirited, do the best you can to bring the world to peace and harmony;
6. Be family-oriented, self-disciplined;
7. Be free-minded. Follow your dreams;
8. Believe in god. God is one;
9. Be supportive to those who need you, be generous;
10. Create your life as a great, adventurous story.

21 century is the time, when people have to come to the point, when positive and optimistic sense and ideas have to get dominant position worldwide.

There is short description on how to paint in the *NeoPopRealist* manner.
Close your eyes for a moment. Lets make faces. Use acrylic on canvas or ink on paper. The line turns to a beautiful eye on the right side of the canvas. Then lips. Nose. Draw left eye that belong to another person and look different then right one. Draw profile that picture right part of the face. Draw nose, lips that belong to another, left part of the face. Add hair, ears, and symbolic objects as a backdrop.
Now color. Feel free, get bold, cold one. Another one, hot. Third, cold one . . . Do you like what you see? Turn on all your senses. Feeling of harmony is important condition. Enjoy process. It is fun, it is game, it is enjoyment. And total satisfaction at the end.
What you see look too simple to you? Make it more complicated: double line, triple line. Connect eyes, nose, lips, ears and figures at the background. Play 'til "drop dead", following your feeling of harmony. Sorry if you do not have it. Then you are in trouble. Important condition is a talent, professional skills, imagination and sharp sense of the contemporary world.

Art develops along with society. We cannot stop its evolutionary movement whether we want to or not. Art always reflects people lives, their economic and cultural achievements, and technical progress. The great artists of the past reflect their own eras, and therefore became part of history. We know the names of Picasso, Dali, Warhol . . . Each of them is a vivid representative of his time, and made his own particular, extraordinary contribution to art.
The 20th century saw the furious battle of two such dramatically opposite styles as Pop Art and Realism. Pop Art was badly received by proponents of Realism. And Pop Art in its turn ignored Realism.

The second half of the 20th century could not ignore Andy Warhol, because he was its vibrant representative. His devotees were not in the minority. There were as numerous as the supporters of realism. Andy Warhol could not be ignored because he was a representative of his time whose art reflected the life of huge numbers of people — their interests, feelings and needs. It does not matter whether we like his art or not. Then came Jeff Koons . . . In the year 2000, it seems that the development of art had reached a dead end. The new millennium demanded something different, new, something that would characterize its new ideas, goals, desires. What could that be?

I was headed this way from the outset. It began more or less in 1989, when I took pen and ink in hand seriously for the first time. I never wanted to imitate the great artists.
Why not be a great artist myself? It is not hard, if you know what you are doing. Without any special art background or skills, deliberately closing all the channels by which artistic information could reach me, I refused to allow my brain to work as a copy machine. I decided to "reinvent the bicycle," more precisely, "bicycles." From December 1989 to 1996, I moved from ink on paper to acrylic on canvas, passing by way of oil on canvas.
The artist is an unusual creature. I can make this claim with certainty because I began to make art seriously at the age of 29. Before that, I was trying to be an ordinary, "normal" person. I worked as a journalist, a musician, tried nearly 10 professions out of boredom. I came to the visual arts, for which I had had an affinity for since childhood.
The visual arts are an abyss, a narcotic. If you enter them, there is no way out. You will be lost to everyone else. What does this mean? Simply that a person has decided to follow his own path, not a group path, but a singular way. For some it is a long road, for others short, and some lose their way in the fog . . .
My artistic experiment consisted of the following: living in a country that had been closed to new trends in art, I decided to invent a new style that would shake the world, as Picasso, Dali, Warhol and a few other great artists had done.
As I already mentioned, I had not received an education in art, but all through childhood I had drawn for elementary, secondary, and then college school newspapers, etc. I had a musical education and was involved with journalism, so I already had experience in experimenting with the brain gray matter. With only 16 percent of it in use during "normal" activities, the brain cannot produce interesting results. If a greater portion of the gray matter comes into play, then one can expect extraordinary results.
How can this be done? It is not all that complicated. That, which makes us ordinary, normal people, makes us bad artists. The conclusion is as follows: forget about every day life, the fact that you belong to some kind of system, walk in line, are supposed to organize relations with people, function within society. Some artists drink to achieve this (but "don't drink and draw!"), others use drugs. My way of approaching it is auto-suggestion. This was difficult in the beginning: I would go "on" and "off", "on" and "off." Now, however, the "on" state has become a constant. This is what it is — to be an artist. The brain is always ready to create unusual pictures that involve the transformation of reality, of the seen and heard, into the language of color and line. It becomes easy and unforced, whereas earlier it involved pain and suffering. It was difficult because professionalism limped along on one leg. And in order to bring a painting to a finished state, it was necessary to undergo a lot of suffering. Harmony and professionalism were not walking in step. The ideal feeling of harmony had insufficient professionalism. Now, when they walk side by side, it has become very easy to call up all sorts of pirouettes, leaps and jumps. Painting has become an entirely pleasurable activity.

I will return now to a discussion of the *NeoPopRealism* style. Where did this name come from? Even my
very early works did not fi t into any exhibitions or any particular gallery. My 1st group exhibit was in 1990 in Moscow's Manege. In answer to the questions "What style do you draw and paint in?" I could not give a definitive answer. That was a dead end for me. I was tired of wracking my brains about how to answer.
In Florida in 2002, I created a series of bright canvases, including "Seasons of Nightmare" (or "Green Face of Greed"), "His Inner" and "Miss & Her Admirer," which formed the finished system of artistic representation in my style. At the time, for that matter, someone commented that they were impossible to copy — and he was correct.
In 2003, I decided to create a word what would characterize my works as much as possible. My paintings are bright, appear to be quite simply made, and at the same time their content is profound. Logically, it seemed, this was Pop Art and Realism together. In addition, I added the particle "Neo." As a result, I ended up with "*NeoPopRealism*," combining Pop Art and Realism.

A little secret. I had many artistic friends in Moscow. I had questions for them about technical matters. But as far as color and other individual matters that characterize an artist individuality, I never wanted to hear their advice. I believed in my feeling of harmony. And I always knew that with an ideal feeling of harmony it is possible to get out of any difficult situation alone on canvas. We are all subject to a higher harmony in this world. Everything else is secondary. If you have a marvelous feeling for harmony, you can spit on the canvas and it will be brilliant. And so, I played with brushes and paints in my own way and relied exclusively on my extravagant contemporaneity and ideal feeling of lack of desire to repeat anything done by any artist I knew or did not know. No matter how great he was. As a result — you are acquainted with *NeoPopRealism*. Forgive me for the "ism." But there was no way around it. I had to give a name to the results of my brazen artistic nihilism. A small detail. As I already mentioned, the history of art is a gradual transformation of styles. I could not have come to *NeoPopRealism* just like that. *NeoPopRealism* is the result of the invention of several "bicycles." It turned out, accidentally, that I live at the beginning of the new millennium. And at this period of time it could have been nothing else but *NeoPopRealism*. Simply because it is precisely this style that fully reflects this era with its silliness and refined intellectuality, with its technological achievements and technical progress, with its social and ethnic, and cultural differences.

Being absolutely unfamiliar with western and American art experiments, between 1989 and 1992, I passed through a transformation beginning with the African style drawings to Andy Warhol bright fl at faces. In between were Dali, Pollock and other representatives of the leading art styles.

I came to the United States for the first time in 1992. And it was a continuation of my personal artistic evolution, which reached its peak in 2002, in Florida.

Because of its elite qualities, visual art is not particularly meaningful or important for the masses if there is not deep philosophy behind it. In the 21st century, the masses are tired of waiting for the end of the world, which has apparently been put off for several hundred years. And for a good life, we need a positive view of reality.

I have created a 21st century philosophy for a better life. In effect, it is the philosophy of the beautiful people and a healthy life, which we should all strive for in order to preserve the world, our individual health (physical and psychological), improve life and strive for perfection. If one follows the canons of *NeoPopRealism,* the individual's life will begin to change in a positive direction. And the place to start is at #1: Be Beautiful. Beauty will save the world, is hardly a new idea. It produces a charge of positive energy. Then we move on to #2: Be creative, never stop studying and learning. Do not fall behind the times, develop yourself, be progressive. #3: Be peace-loving and positive-minded. If you are inclined toward the positive you will attract positive people. And your life will change, will be transformed into pleasure, and so on . . . The 10 canons of *NeoPopRealism* are the key to making your life flourishing and successful. And that means they are the key to complete satisfaction. The 21st century has its own laws. And if we do not heed them, we can end up in a difficult situation, which has already led to enormous catastrophes and tragedies. We need art, beauty, and positive thinking . . .

Additional books by NeoPopRealismPRESS, published in 2011:

1. How to Draw NeoPopRealism Ink Images: Basics, ISBN: 9780615515755 (for teens/adults)

2. Как выполнять НеоПопРеалистический рисунок тушью: Основы, ISBN: 9780615516967 (for teens/adults)

3. How to draw Without Eraser: Children's Guide to the World of NeoPopRealism, ISBN: 9780615521824

4. УЧИТЕСЬ РИСОВАТЬ БЕЗ РЕЗИНКИ: гид для детей в мир НеоПопРеализма, ISBN: 9780615523484

5. How to Draw NeoPopRealism Abstract Images: Ink Backgrounds, ISBN: 9780615527437 (for teens/adults)

6. How to Draw NeoPopRealism Abstract Images: Metallic Exuberance, ISBN: 978-0615560991(for teens/adults)

7. Black Book for NeoPopRealism Metallic INK pen Drawing, ISBN: 978-0615561028 (for everyone)

8. How to Draw Advanced NeoPopRealism Ink Images, ISBN: 978-0615569758 (for teens/adults)

9. How to Draw NeoPopRealism Color Abstract Images: Ink Backgrounds, ISBN: 978-0615579559 (for teens/adults)

10. How to Draw the NeoPopRealism Abstract: Children's Guide, ISBN: 978-0615545332

11. Fort Lauderdale 100: A Must-Have Collector's Edition, ISBN: 9780615470085 (English with partial translation in Russian)

12. Fort Lauderdale 100: Reflections: A Must-Have Collector's Edition, ISBN: 978-0615554464

13. Fort Lauderdale 100: Yachting Capital: A Must-Have Collector's Edition, ISBN: 978-0615562223

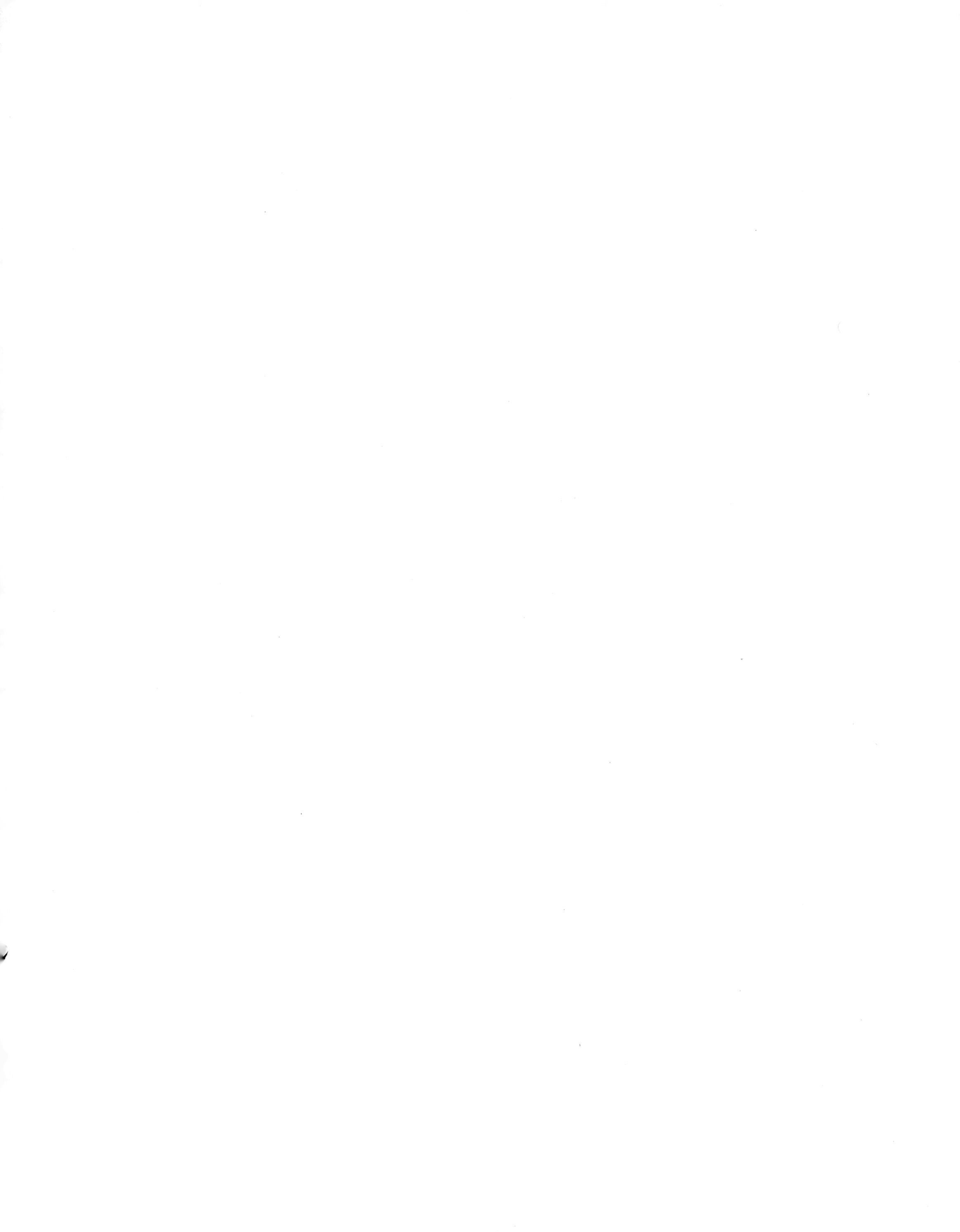

First time published in 2010

Reprinted with the minor changes in 2012 by NeoPopRealism PRESS
PO BOX 366
New York, NY 10013

NeoPopRealismPRESS@mail.com

NeoPopRealism Starz: 21st Century ART, Erotica As A High Artistic Aspiration
by Nadia Russ

ISBN-13: 978-0615621555
ISBN-10: 0615621554

12 13 14 15 16   10 9 8 7 6 5 4 3 2 1

Published in the United States of America
Language: English

This book explores the history of erotica in visual arts and includes images of the artwork from contemporary artists from all over the globe.

www.neopoprealism.org

www.ingramcontent.com/pod-product-compliance
Lightning Source LLC
LaVergne TN
LVHW070146110826
845147LV00002B/333
* 9 7 8 0 6 1 5 6 2 1 5 5 5 *